LEX MUSKETEERS

VOLUME I

ADVOCATE AMARDEEP SINGH CHANDOK

Contents

DISCLAIMER

Neither the Lex Muskeeters, consisting of the articles of the different authors including images (if any) nor its editors, publishers, owners or anyone else involved in creating, producing or delivering the book or material contained therein, assumes any responsibility for the accuracy, usefulness or correctness etc of the views of the different writers. The role of lex muskeeters is only up to providing a platform to the different writers for development of the habit of writing and reading.

The opinions, discussions, views are the independent thoughts of the writers and the editor or the owner makes no warranty, express or implied, with respect the material contained therein. The owner or the editors will not be liable for any direct, indirect, consequential, special, exemplary or other damages arising therefrom.

Lex Muskeeters

Lex Muskeeters is a project of Book Adopters Foundation, primarily working in the field of spread of education. The term 'lex' refers to the system or the body of laws and the term 'muskeeters' refers to a soldier armed with a musket. The collective meaning of the term "Lex Muskeeters" refers to a soldier having the arm of law.

The prime objective of the book is to provide a platform to all the persons, who are interested in writing with specific reference to law but not limited to laws only. This book is an endeavour to cover all the norms of the nature, society and commands of the soverign in general through the words of the different ideologies and experts of the different fields. Apart from that the lex muskeeters also provide an opportunity to the layman to express his feelings and experiences towards the social aspects of the norms with aim to provide a reference to the researchers.

BOOK ADOPTERS FOUNDATION

This foundation is one of its own kind of organization, with unique aim to spread the education and to re-develop the habit of reading books with its motto that "Proper Utilization of a Book is our Paramount Consideration." This foundation is started by six intellectual personalities under the vision of Advocate Amardeep Singh Chandok, with five other persons namely Advocate Harsh Jindia, Advocate Manjit Singh, Advocate Hiten Gupta, Advocate Hemant Sharma and Mr. Tarun Sharma. This organization is growing since its inception and successfully got various donors of the books and a thousand of readers in the locality.

I

Law of Attraction. [Author: Adv. A.S. Chandok]

Broadly speaking about "Law"; it is what the different jurists told about it. The actual phenomena lie in the definition of Law. Sometimes, it is the command of the sovereign and sometimes, it came out of the common consciousness of the persons or the society at large. Law is basically a set of rules decided by the sovereign through the legislature or the precedent for the smooth functioning of the society in a proper manner.

Law is either substantial or the procedural; when it came forward to provide rights and duties, it is termed as substantial but at the same time when provides the process for achieving the ultimate goals then it is coined as the procedural one. Apart from all these technical norms, there is always the existence of the grundnorm i.e. the base of all the law, which may either, be the constitution or the king.

The above captioned forms of the law are generally considered as the forms of the man made law. As we all know, there is a supreme power beyond the limits of the mankind and we termed it as the nature or the almighty.

If we have to discuss the law of nature in our routine life, we can see that

- The day came after the night.
- The summer came after the winter.
- The rotation of the earth.
- The gravity of the land.
- The whisper of the birds with the daylight.
- The rise of the sun.
- The attraction of the magnet etc.

We often call these terms as the universal laws. After getting inspiration from all these laws, I want to discuss here about one of the greatest law of the universe that is the law of the nature, which did not have any sanction of the man made law or in other words we can say that neither codified nor in the limits of the man to define. But it still persists in the nature like the light and air. This law is called the law of attraction.

On the casual side we can say that this law is also identified by the bollywood in the movie "Om Shanti Om" when SRK says that

"Agar Kisi Cheez ko dil sa Chaho

To Puri Qayinat usey tumse

milane ki koshish ma Lag Jaati hai"

if we see the practical aspect of the attraction, it really works. But the only thing which it demands is the consistency and dedication. Being the basic law of the universe, it brings positivity in life and bars the negative waves to enter the mindset of the mankind.

If we go thoroughly in the concept, we can feel that a man can do anything with the power of attraction. If we go back to the earlier Era's of mankind, no one can even think to fly with the help of planes. But now, with dedication and by the virtue of the power of attraction the man has also built up the rockets and satellites to go beyond the limits of the planet earth. This happens only due to the continuous attraction of the persons to look after the sky.

The power of attraction can also be utilized by the aspirants preparing for exams and you can see that the results are magical. The divine authority will help the person who shows a little dedication with the means of attraction. The most important question which came to one's mind is, "if the law of attraction is so powerful, then what is the need to work hard?" one just have to attract and he will get it.

The answer to this question is the prime factor behind the law of attraction is the dedication; one has to put little efforts to make the things more favorable. For example, if we look at a stamp, the words engraved in the stamp are exactly opposite to the final print, one just have to put a little efforts to ink the stamp to make the words shine.

For the sake of contention, we can also consider that the nature provide the sufficient means of eating for all of it creatures. On the same hand the nature did not feed the creature by itself, one just has to put a little effort to find the meal and to chew it. Everything is available in our surrounding. But one has to put efforts to make it worthy and this is termed in the words as the power of attraction. This power is very similar to the power of magnet. If we attract with consistency and dedication it attracts like the opposite poles of the magnate, on the other hand if one fails to put the continuous efforts, then it throws the thing away like the same poles of the magnate.

So keep attracting what you want to achieve.

II

Violating The Dead: A Study on Legal Framework of Necrophilia in India. [Author: Chitrarekha Bharadwaj]

Globally, the criminal justice system is progressive, dynamic and evolutionary and interacts with a wide range of potential emerging social problems. Criminal jurisprudence's primary purpose is to identify and eradicate various social ills. Necrophilia is one such infamous and contentious topic. The phrase refers to the odd behaviour of necrophilia, which is the attraction and desire for a corpse or dead body. Many nations fail to even recognise this problem and lack the appropriate regulations to deal with it. The State is unable to prosecute and punish the accused involved in such an act because of this legal incapacity. Necrophilia cases in India are on the rise, but tragically there is no law in place to control this regrettable conduct.

However, in the case of **State v. Ryan1**, a paradigm shift has finally developed with relation to necrophilia. Following this case, other States began to take steps to make necrophilia a crime and regarded the behaviour as being wrong. This behaviour not alone offends the grieving kin it also violates society standards in that it is against ethics to treat the deceased with anything other than respect and dignity**2**.

However, the COVID-19 pandemic came as a bolt out of the blue and contributed to the high mortality toll which resulted in the dumping and improper disposal of corpses in rivers and remote areas in various states. The probability of horrible crimes against the dead, such as necrophilia, has increased due to the difficulty to properly dispose of human remains.

Necrophilia has additionally been classified as a psychiatric condition, alongside other disorders that are primarily sexual in nature, such as masochism and paedophilia. Given the grisly nature of the crime and its impact or better put, unfavourable impact—on society's conscience, it becomes essential to criminalise it, something that numerous legal authorities across many different countries have neglected to accomplish.

Thus, the dilemma of whether necrophilia constitutes a crime or, as many indicate, an illness that calls for therapy rather than punishment, emerges. While natural law theorists view an act that breaches the moral and ethical code as guilt, positivists see crime as a human invention. Necrophilia, on the other hand, meets the criteria for both of these ideas and is thus a crime. Additionally, recognising necrophilia as a misdemeanour would be in keeping with stated goal of criminal law of protecting rights of individuals.

MEANING AND CLASSIFICATION

Necrophilia in very simple terms refers to "an act of a person engaging in sexual activity with a corpse". It is considered as Paraphilia by the World Health Organization and state "necrophilia as a condition characterised by abnormal sexual desires, typically involving extreme or dangerous activities that can have further dangerous repercussions"[3]. It derives from two distinct Greek terms, nekros and philia, which mean "dead" and "love", respectively, and when put together simply means "love with the dead".

Additionally, the Court of Criminal Appeals said in the 1973 case of **Locke v. State[4]**, that the act of Necrophilia is the "*most loathsome, degrading and vile sexual activity imaginable*"[5].

The earliest recorded use of this word appears in Joseph Guislain's writings, where he refers to "Necrophiles as patients rather than criminals" and presents necrophilia as a condition that may be treated rather than an offence that has to be suppressed[6].

It took a while for the act of necrophilia to come to light and for a definition to be established, but it has eventually be done. Some specialists consider it to be a serious medical issue, and Dr. Anil Agrawal additionally suggested that there are several types of necrophilia. He also developed ten-tier taxonomy of necrophilia based on his vast study on the subject[7]. For the purpose of this study, the focus is only on the three categories –

1. Regular Necrophiles - Those who fall into this category of Necrophiles can be considered to be true Necrophiles because they do not experience any sexual or sensual pleasure while performing physical intimacy with the deceased and are only interested in having a submissive partner they can control and possess rather than being concerned with sentiments of bonding.

2. Homicidal Necrophiles - The most notorious examples of such homicidal Necrophiles include Jeffrey Dahmer and Dennis Nilsen, who each killed a large number of victims to satiate their lust. This classification can be regarded as the most disturbed one because the individuals falling within this classification are the most horrifying ones because they murderothers in order to satisfy their sexual appetite and may also be discovered to be involved in bizarre act of cannibalism.

3. Fantasy Necrophiles – This group of people includes necrophiliacs, or those who just construct castles in their heads when it comes to the physical closeness that a cadaver or corpse elicits in them. It is not required that they will really engage in this behavior; they may occasionally only fantasize about it.

There are other classifications as well like romantic Necrophiles, tactile Necrophiles, opportunistic Necrophiles, role players, fetishist Necrophiles, Necromutilomaniacs and exclusive Necrophiles.

Although the third group poses no immediate threat to society, the other division cannot be stated to be in the same light. Both the first and second categories have the potential to "shake the collective conscience of the society", and as a result, they must face legal repercussions.

NECROPHILIA & PSYCHOLOGY

Numerous healthcare professionals have attempted to understand the underlying cause and clinical justification of necrophilia using a great deal of research, data, and statistics. As per their investigation, the well-known rationale they discovered is "low confidence and apprehension about dismissal" as made sense by Rosman and Resnick[8]. Psychologists consider that Necrophiles view dead corpses as sex objects that won't rebel against them or reject them, and because of this, they will really want to retain their confidence.

The major theme in necrophilia is a substantial lack of self-assurance and well- established feelings of unworthiness and unexpected vulnerability to dismissal. As a result, they look for a suitable companion to satiate their erotic longings

who is never capable of dismissing them. The defence element of responsive growth, which replaces an unacceptable propensity with its opposite, causes individuals to become fascinated by the deceased and obsessed on them even if they may initially be unpleasant of the dead.

Further, some experts are of the opinion that many Necrophiles are motivated by the inherent serial killers tendencies to brutally kill their victims and then have physical relation with the corpse in order to reassure their condescending nature. Ted Bundy is a classical example of such condescending and pervert nature as he used to visit the graves for his victims and sit there for long hours after the homicide and enjoy the experience again in his mind.

As a result, drawing generalisations regarding the mental health of Necrophiles is difficult, and it is impossible to say that all Necrophiles are motivated by some sort of mental condition.NECROPHILIA: A **HISTORICAL BACKGROUND**

Perversity has always been regarded as the abhorrent embodiment of evil and has always represented the dark side of sexuality as it is sinful, wicked, corrupt, and immoral and a crime calling for harsh punitive measures. The act of Necrophilia is not a new concept and had been practiced since ages but always remained dormant and unheard.

While turning the pages of history, it appears that sexual intercourse with the corpses was a known concept and despised by the ancient Egyptians. **Herodotus**, the Father of History, in his celebrated writing - **The Histories**, quoted *"When the wife of a distinguished man dies, or any woman who happens to be beautiful or well known, her body is not given to the embalmers immediately, but only after the lapse of three or four days. This is a precautionary measure to prevent the embalmers from violating her corpse, a thing which is actively said to have happened in the case of a woman who had just died".***9**

Although, the treatment for male corpses was different as "pseudo-copulation" ritual was performed with the carcass with the belief that it will restore the virility (masculinity) of dead man**10**. Another classical demonstration for the existence of Necrophilia in ancient times is the **Luo** (a community of Kenya and Tanzania) of East Africa who had the belief that the ghost of a virgin female was terribly menacing and should be appeased by deflowering her corpse by a stranger**11**.

Further, some professionals in the field interpreted that the *"curse of pharaoh's tomb"* folklore was fashioned with the purpose to outmanoeuvre the acts of necrophilia. It is believed that the strong marble covering on the tomb were profoundly done with the rationale to protect the sanctity of the dead person and to keep the perpetrators away from the violating the dead and let them rest in peace.

The term 'Necrophilia' was coined by Belgian psychiatrist Joseph Guislain in the year 1850. However, the term was not in fashion at that time and got recognition almost fifty years later of its inception in 1894 **12**. Richardvon Krafft- Ebing in the year 1894 used the term 'Necrophilia' in a wider sense by publishing his work "Psychopathic Sexualize" among the masses and demonstrated his idea of Necrophilia as *"horrible manifestation of sadism"***13**. Further, in 1941, the masses accepted the perspective of Abraham A. Bill who demonstrated Necrophiles as *"mentally deficient and psychotic people"*.

Moving further to the contemporary period, there are many infamous, notorious examples of Necrophiles. One of such example is the British serial killer Jeffrey Dahmer, who was fantasized with sex slave and wanted a submissive partner, so decided to kill the people he liked, preserved their bodies and had erotic relationship with them until the corpse got decomposed beyond recognition.

The very recent development regarding Necrophilia can be found in the book *"Necrophilia: Forensic and Medico-Legal Aspects"* authored by Dr. Anil Agrawal in which he focused on explaining the categories of Necrophiles. This book can be considered as the first ever publication or text on Necrophilia. In this book, he inspected a general scientific, psychological, historical and social perspective of act of Necrophilia by focusing primarily on its contributing factors and cogent theories. Hence, the concept of Necrophilia is not new to the society; it had been prevalent since ages as unheard and ignorant act because no one paid much heed to protect the rights of dead.

INTERNATIONAL PERSPECTIVE ON NECROPHILIA

The alarming increase in the number of cases of Necrophilia is a topic of concern and is a poorly understood phenomenon and even less discussed topic. The absence of legislation for the offence of act of Necrophilia is a gap in the existing legislation and in order to fill this gap, the foremost priority is to take into consideration the views of worldwide communities.

The act of Necrophilia is not new and its practice was prevalent at archaic times and was made illegal in many countries. The countries criminalized the act of Necrophilia on the ground of being it violative of dignity of the dead as well as privacy of the dead. Further, in order to build legislation, the views and opinions of international community must be considered and comparable

modification of rules may pave the way in many ways to fill the gap in the legislation by updating the law on regular basis.

Many universal laws out rightly expresses the rights of the dead and their privileges and some are mentioned below –

- The Cairo Presentation on Human Rights in Islam, 1990 under Article 3(a) provides that *"in case of the utilization of power and in the event equipped clash it is denied to ravage the dead bodies"*.
- Furthermore, the United States Field Manual, 1956 states that *"abuse of the dead bodies is an atrocity"* and the United States Maritime Handbook, 1995 clearly provides that the abuse, vandalization and mutilation of the dead is the characterization of war crimes and violation of human rights which cannot be legitimized.
- Further, the recent development in regards to the rights of dead is a resolution passed in 2005 by the United Nations Commission on Human Rights and Forensic Science which highlighted *"the importance of dignified handling of human remains, including their proper management and disposal as well as respect of respect for the needs of families"*.

The above-mentioned universal pledges provide the reverence and veneration for the rights of dead and hold the core value of human rights laws as it highlights the significance of manoeuvring of human remains which makes the member States binding to legislate a law to effectuate their respective international obligations.

Some States in this regards enacted penal provisions to establish the penal liability for the act of Necrophilia but are vague in nature and implementation.

United States of America - The practise of necrophilia is not specifically addressed by any law in the United States of America as a crime; instead, it is up to the individual States in the country to enact their own laws on the matter. Only a handful States of United States of America officially address the conduct of necrophilia in their criminal laws, which often deal with crimes involving dead bodies or corpses. These States are Georgia, Arizona, Hawaii, and Rhode Island. Four of them expressly define, and give the punishment for the term "Necrophilia" in their respective statutes. Necrophilia penalty varies from State to State, for instance, in Georgia; it can result in a jail sentence of one year to fifteen years.

United Kingdom - As per the Section 70 of the Sexual Offences Act, 2003 of United Kingdom provides the criminalization of the act of sexual intercourse to a corpse and prescribes a punishment of imprisonment for a term which should not exceed two years . However, by contemplating the statistics and records, it is asserted that there is no prosecution in UK for the offence of Necrophilia[14].

In the case of **State v. Ryan**[15], the accused broke into the cemetery twice within a week and damaged the property as well as harmed the sanctity of the dead by making sexual contact with the corpse. The Court of Appeal of Washington upheld the conviction imposed by the trial Court of imposition of an exceptional sentence, however, the accused was not charged for the act of Necrophilia as his contact with the corpse was reportedly not a felony at the time he violated into the crematorium. Subsequent to the conviction of Ryan, a bill was introduced and passed in the legislature making the act of Necrophilia illegal[16].

Canada - The act of Necrophilia in Canada is illegal and penalized as per the provisions of Section 182 of the Criminal Code of Canada, 1985 which explicitly use the term "Necrophilia" and states that *"anyone who acts lewdly or inappropriately or proposes humiliation to or remains of a deceased body shall be liable of a crime of and shall be liable to incarceration for a period not more than five years"*.

France - It is indeed strange to see France's position on necrophilia, given it is said that ghost marriage -marrying a dead body or corpse—is more ancient than the "Magna Carta" itself. Necrogamy, the posthumous union of a living person with a deceased person, is a peculiar ritual that is practiced in France. According to the requirements of Article 171 of French Civil Code, such necrophilia is permissible in France[17].

Despite the similarities in wording between the Indian and Canadian rules, the Canadian provision is more inclusive and applies to everyone, whereas the Indian legislation only applies to those who have intruded on the place of burial. Additionally, the penalty is five times larger under Canadian law than it is under Indian law.

CONSTITUIONAL PERSPECTIVE VIS-A-VIS NECROPHILIA

Constitution is the grundnorm of our country as it is the reverent and paramount source of law and the municipal laws acquire their legality, relevancy and applicability from the grundnorm. Therefore, the question regarding the legal status of a dead body can only be answered by putting prominence on the startling argument on legal status of the dead body *vis-à-vis* rights reserved for dead in the Constitution of India. The answer to this dubious question lies in the grey area and provides an unsatisfactory answer in the present legal jurisprudence in India. However, the altar the justice, the Supreme Court from time and again maintained and upheld the reverence and dignity of the dead in plethora of judicial pronouncements by the virtue of Article 21 of the Constitution.

The Supreme Court in the landmark case of **Paramananda Katara v. Union of India**[18] held that *"the Article 21 of the Constitution* *casts the obligation on the State to preserve life and extends it not only to the living but also to his dead body".*

Further, the Supreme Court reiterated the same in the case of **Ramji Singh Mujeeb v. State of Uttar Pradesh & Ors.19,** and stated that the horizon of Article 21 ensures the right to dignity to the dead as well. The same view was opined by the Supreme Court in the case of **Amrutha v. State of Kerala20,** where Court quoted *"even dead person have got the right of privacy under the ambit of Article 21 and their souls should not be disturbed as they have immortal life after their death".*

Further, Justice Prafulla Chandra Pant, former Chairperson of National Human Rights Commission, a short while ago, advocated for the enactment of law to protect the sanctity and dignity of a dead body and advanced that right to fair treatment and protection of dignity extends not only to a living person but also to their dead bodies. It is the duty of the State to protect the sanctity and rights of the deceased either the death is natural or unnatural.

Moreover, despite the plethora of judicial pronouncements and plenty of guidelines issued by different authorities, the Criminal Legal System in India shrugged a cold shoulder as far as the legal status of a dead is concerned. Further, the State turned a blind eye to enact a provision under the penal code consistent with the principles of the Indian Constitution to prevent the violation of rights of the dead due to the vagueness and ambiguity in the Indian Criminal Justice System. Hence, by observing the principles enshrined under the 2005 resolution and the judicial pronouncements which provides for the rights of the dead regarding the dignified handling of the corpse, the act of Necrophilia, in this regards befits as an act of vandalism against the dead and not a sexual attack.

LEGISLATIVE FRAMEWORK ON NECROPHILIA: A CRITICAL APPRAISAL

Nearly every nation in the world has laws prohibiting Necrophilia, despite the fact that it is hardly known in India. Some are strong, while others are hazy and unclear. India ranks lowest within the latter group of nations because its legislative reforms are less transparent than those in other nations.

In India, only two sections of the Indian Penal Code, 1860 now address crimes involving dead bodies; however they do not specifically address acts of necrophilia. These provisions are Sections 297 and 377 of the Indian Penal Code, 1860; nevertheless they were created for other offences that damage the rights of the deceased rather than specifically dealing with the crime of necrophilia.

However, considering the numerous forms of necrophilia that are pervasive in society, it is challenging for the police to cite these two sections. Also these provisions have many loopholes due to which the accused cannot be convicted under Section 297 and 377 of the Indian Penal Code, 1860.

Section 297 of the Indian Penal Code, 1860 states that *"whoever, with the intention of wounding the feelings of any person, or of insulting the religion of any person, or with the knowledge that the feelings of any person are likely to be wounded, or that the religion of any person is likely to be insulted thereby, commits any trespass in any place of worship or on any place of sepulchre, or any place set apart from the performance of funeral rites or as a depository for the remains of the dead, or offers any indignity to any human corpse, or causes disturbance to any persons assembled for the performance of funeral ceremonies, shall be punished with imprisonment of either description for a term which may extend to one year, or with fine, or with both"*.

Hence, conforming to the provisions of the Section 297 of the Indian Penal Code, 1860, it demonstrates the idea that in order to bring shame to the dead, one has to meddle into cemetery and such meddling will conform to the idea of trespass in graveyard and will come within the purview of necrophilia. As a result, this arrangement of the provision protects the person who engages in the act of necrophilia without actually setting foot in a cemetery from the jurisdiction of Indian Law.

The main challenge in proving any instance of necrophilia underneath this provision is meeting the prerequisite, namely, trespassing into a burial ground, which is often not met since the offender has not really trespassed. The same is true whether the accused killed the victim only for the purpose of taking the corpse or if the offence was conducted at another location where no trespassing took place.

With the aforementioned rules, there are several restrictions since even if someone is discovered performing one of the forbidden activities in the sections, they cannot be charged under the section. For instance, if someone is there in an official role, they cannot be held accountable. This is because the accused did not trespass, which is the very first requirement of the abovementioned provision. The sentence of one year in jail for such a serious offence, which affects society as a whole and also breaches the section's basic guarantee of a respectful burial, has no significant inhibitory effect on the violation.

There have been several claims made by families in India in recent years that the dead bodies of their loved ones were polluted by Dieners during the night, but none of them have been confirmed because there is no supporting proof.

There is no law in India that requires such wrongdoers to be put on trial, regardless of whether the accusations were proven.

Further, Section 377 of the Indian Penal Code, 1860 provides that *"whoever voluntarily has carnal intercourse against the order of nature with any man, woman or animal shall be punished with imprisonment for life, or with imprisonment of either description for a term which may extend to ten years, and shall also be liable to fine."*

Insofar as it rises issues related to gay relationships, this section has been the subject of a protracted dispute. The Hon'ble Apex Court in the case of **Navtej Singh Johar v. Union of India**21 decriminalized the homosexual consensual relationship. Three requirements must be met in order to penalize someone under this provision, and they are – 1) involuntary intercourse, 2) against the order of the nature, 3) with any man or woman or animal.

A typical example of necrophilia only satisfies two requirements, and the current Indian legal system has yet to acknowledge the requirement that the act was performed voluntarily. It is impractical to judge whether an encounter was consensual or forced in situations of necrophilia. If it is feasible to ascertain the dead's permission, rape or sexual assault would unquestionably be committed. However, whether or not a deceased person can grant permission depends on how the issue is understood.

Due to the requirement that the intercourse be "against the order of nature" the other two requirements of the section are absolutely satisfied. The terms "unnatural offences" and "against the order of nature" are ill-defined and ambiguous because there is no clear definition, but thanks to the interpretation of the "Victorian Principle", any sexual act that does not lead to procreation is considered to be unnatural, and necrophilia cases very well fall under this category because they do not produce offspring.

Finally, Section 10 of the IPC defines "man" as a male human being of any age and "woman" as a "female" human being of any age in the third essential. Following the death of the individual, a human body continues to be 'human', and hence section 377 may be applied after they have become quasi-subjects before the law. To get over the inconsistency in the provision and effectively incorporate the crime of necrophilia inside it, a small change to this section is required.

Further, some psychologists claim that Necrophilia is a Paraphilia which makes the Necrophile, a mentally unstable person. Such interpretation will provide the accused an escape from the penal punishment if he commits the act of Necrophilia as will get the defence of insanity. The study reveals that the homicidal Necrophiles not only commit the act of Necrophilia but perform a series of events that make them commit 'n' number of crimes like trespassing, killing, necrophilia and then cannibalism in some cases. Such act does not only concern the rights of the dead but affects the society at large and comes within the purview of "rarest of the rare case".

Criminals convicted in the case of "rarest of the rare" cases are not subject to defence of insanity, then why should Necrophiles escape the liability using the same, when their act is in parlance to that of a criminal who committed "rarest of the rare" crime and is equivocal in nature.

When criminals have been unable to gain control of another person's body, their necrophiliac tendency has served as their primary source of motivation. One can easily envision the increased level of cruelty and inhumanity exhibited by such a culprit. In addition to being very ambiguous in this respect, Indian law is also the cause for the increased cases for such heinous conduct and is high time to modify the present laws or enact a new one.

JUDICIAL APPROACH TOWARDS NECROPHILIA

There have been numerous Necrophilia events and cases throughout the years, but the problem hasn't yet been brought to public attention in a way that would make it go away. Necrophilia-related legislation has not received much attention from legislators, despite the growth of laws. India's circumstances are the same. However, the most heinous example of necrophilia, murder, and cannibalism, known as the "Nithari Case", resurfaced in 2006. This case raises the issue of whether or not the rise of necrophilia instances in India will result in legislation that deal just with that type of crime. In spite of this, the situation is still the same 16 years after the Nithari Case.

Nithari case - The Nithari Case[22] was referred to as "the rarest of rare cases in India's history." The story gained attention in 2006 when two sweepers in Noida discovered eight skeletons in a sewer. There were two suspects in this case: Moninder Singh Pandher (the owner of the house), and Surinder Koli, who worked as his domestic helper. Since there were several reports of children going missing from a nearby town, the inquiry was led to Pandher's home, which is why the case has received so much media attention. In this case's inquiry, the police had indeed acted carelessly, so the CBI was given control of the matter afterwards.

In 2007, the two suspects were detained by CBI for 14 days in order to conduct a narcotics analysis. Following this, the CBI handed Pandher a clean bill of health; however, accused Surinder

Koli admitted to the crime, was declared to be a cannibal, and was accused of raping a 20-year-old female. Accused Koli was indicted of raping, killing, and kidnapping at least 19 minors as well as one adult. In 2009, the trial court imposed the death punishment on both of the defendants after several charge sheets were submitted against Koli. The execution order issued by the trial court was also upheld by the Allahabad High Court.

However, the Supreme Court in 2012 suspended the death sentences of both the accused. And Koli received several other punishments under different charges of murder, rape and cannibalism. However, in 2014, the Supreme Court categorically denied the plea of accused for a reconsideration of the death penalty, declaring that the court had not erred in issuing the ruling. Consequently, after all of this time passed, he was handed a death sentence in 2019 after his 10th conviction, but he hasn't been condemned to death yet and is still incarcerated in Tihar prison.

The following are some of the heartbreaking Necrophilia incidents that have surfaced in India in recent years:

- A disturbing and horrible event that occurred as recently as May 2020 and included a lifeless 14-year-old girl who was sexually assaulted by a 50-year-old Assamese man came to light. Akan Saikia, the accused, was a daily labourer who had two wives when the unusual episode was recorded in Arunachal Pradesh. The accused was charged with violating Sections 306 (suicide attempt) and 377 (unnatural offences) of the Indian Penal Code, 1860, as well as Section 8 of the POSCO Act.**23**
- In June 2019, the police detained 42-year-old man from West Bengal, named, Kamruzzaman Sarkar for the crime of killing at least seven women and engaging in sexual activity with their corpses. Along with the murder allegation, he was also accused of hurting and attempting to kill a number of other people over the course of the previous five months. "Sarkar displayed necrophiliac tendencies - so far, we have found that he had sex at least with two women immediately after killing them, and also

inserted foreign objects inside their genitals, says East Burdwan SP Bhaskar Mukherjee"**24**.

Based on their investigation, the authorities came to the conclusion that he used the same method in each case, approaching the victim's home and posing as an electricity department employee to ask permission to check the electric meter before attacking, killing, and having sex with the body of the victim. Later, he grabbed expensive items from his house and fled to make it seem like a robbery narrative. The accused then charged under Section 302 for murder, Section 307 for attempt to murder and Section 376 for committing rape under the Indian Penal Code, 1860.

Therefore, in this recent case, it is evident that the offender was logged for the offence of rape, which is a different offence with a different object, due to a flaw in the legal system and the lack of statutory principles for the act of necrophilia. This cannot be viewed as a modification that frequently work in best interest of the defendant and chastise the alleged perpetrator.

- Another episode involving a 20-year-old factory worker from Gurugram came to light in 2018 when he admitted to having raped numerous of his victims' dead bodies. He had a history of murdering innocent people before having sex with their corpses in order to sate his need**25**.

All these cases explain the urgent requirement to legislate the provisions to deal with the cases of Necrophilia, as in the above-mentioned cases the offenders were not charged specifically for the act of Necrophilia and escape the liability for such a heinous crime.

CONCLUSION & WAY FORWARD

It would therefore be very difficult to deal with cases of necrophilia; making development in the regulation of such bizarre acts of necrophilia by way of legislating appropriate enactments is very needful in the country right now. However, before that, the psychological underpinnings of psyche of Necrophiles ought to be studied in order to understand the psychiatry of such Necrophiles. Furthermore, the creation of robust and efficient regulations and processes is the sole crucial and essential step that can rescue mankind.

The issue of the dignity of the dead is in dispute since Indian law does not provide any specific laws addressing necrophilia. This idea is not new, but it needs to be promptly considered. Necrophilia is currently considered as a contentious issue across the world since different nations have strange and inconsistent laws pertaining to it.

However, some countries, like France and Egypt, have already made necrophilia legal. It is also quite intriguing that some people think Egypt is adopting a legislation that would allow a man to have "farewell intercourse" with his wife up to six hours after she passes away. However, in India, there is no law to charge an offender for the act of Necrophilia, due to which the dignity of the dead remains questionable and can be addressed by following ways –

- The act of Necrophilia should not only be viewed with the respect of the dead but its effect on the society should also be checked. In order to satisfy their passion and sexual fantasies, it contains a number of crimes, including trespassing on cemeteries, kidnapping, and in some horrifying cases, murder, which requires urgent amendments in the present law by recognizing the act as illegal which can be done by modifying the Section 377 of the Indian Penal Code or adding a separate provision for the same.
- The State needs to clarify and expand the legal status and scope of the rights of the dead as right to life also includes right to live with human dignity under Article 21 of the Constitution.
- There must be a mechanism in place for the creation of a Council, which will be responsible for reviewing and analysing the process put in place to regulate the act of necrophilia as well as focusing on the creation of awareness programmes because it's critical to educate people so they can recognise any of these

symptoms.

- • Another crucial issue is how police authorities are trained. They must be taught how to interact with those who have a necrophiliac propensity without upsetting the peace in society and also to provide proper burial or cremation to the neglected bodies.

Hence, there is a continuous need to evaluate the changes in this particular field as well as open the doors to conduct ample research on this unheard issue and making people aware about this bizarre act which is prevalent in society about no one knows about.

III

Domestic Violence against Men. [Author: Ravneet Kaur]

Domestic violence is any type of behaviour used or threatened to be used to control an intimate partner. Threat and control are the two most important elements. Domestic violence can appear in a number of ways:

1. **Physical** -This can include slapping, pushing, or hitting the husband by the wife, her parents, or relatives, as well as throwing objects such as utensils, cell phones, and crockery at him. Slapping was identified as the most common form of physical violence (98.3%) and beaten with a weapon (3.3%). Physical assaults were only severe in one-tenth of the cases.

2. **Sexual relationships** that are compelled upon one partner by the other are included here.This can occur if the husband denies having sex.A study by Malik and Nadda found that only 0.4% of men had been abused sexually.

3. **Psychological** - Consists of a variety of actions, including intimidating the victim, excluding them from friends and family,

controlling where they go, making them feel guilty or crazy, and making unreasonable demands.In emotional abuse against men, it was noted that criticism made up 85% of the abuse, public insults made up 29.7%, and physical threats or injury made up 3.5%. Additionally, it can take the form of mental abuse, such as persistent threats against the husband and his family based on untrue claims of dowry and domestic abuse.

4. **Emotional**-Undermining someone's sense of worth through uncompromising criticism, insults, put-downs, and name-calling.

5. **Economic** - Examples include denying the victim access to family income, forbidding or compelling the victim to work, destroying the victim's property, and controlling all financial decisions.

Domestic violence can affect both women and men. Approximately 1 in 4 women and 1 in 7 men over the age of 18 have experienced physical domestic violence, and nearly 50% of both sexes have gone through some type of domestic psychological aggression, according to statistics from the National Domestic Violence Hotline.

What domestic violence against men looks like in other countries?

In the United States of America, one in every nine males is subjected to domestic abuse by their intimate partner or spouse. One in every seven males has been physically abused by their spouses or intimate partners.

Two out of every five victims of domestic violence in the UK are male. This disproves the widespread misconception that domestic violence only affects women. Men's rights advocacy group Parity claims that most cases of domestic violence against men go unreported and are not typically followed up on by the police.

In Australia, one in every sixteen males has experienced domestic abuse from their spouses, intimate partners, or roommates since the age of 15, whether it took the form of physical or sexual torture.

How frequent are these domestic abuse cases involving Indian men, then? Here are some shocking statistics and information:

1. A survey of 1000 married men in rural Haryana communities found that 52.4% of them experienced gender-based violence. The men's ages ranged from 21 to 49.

2. The most common type of marital or domestic violence against males is emotional abuse (51.6%), with physical abuse coming in second (6%).

3. Low family income, a middle class education, living in a nuclear family, and an offender under the influence of alcohol were risk factors.

4. Over the course of their lives, 51.5% of men have experienced torture or abuse at the hands of their spouses or other close relationships.

5. The general stereotypes against men, the worry of fabricated cases, societal and familial pressure, and denial are the four most frequent reasons why domestic violence cases against Indian men go unreported.

6. While women are more likely than men to consider suicide, men are more likely to die by suicide.

7. The number of beatings by Indian wives of their husbands is third in the world. Those in first and second place are respectively Egypt and the United Kingdom.

8. According to Section 498A of the Indian Penal Code 1860, only a man can be held responsible for cruelty to his wife. There is no provision or clause in the law that makes a woman liable for domestic abuse.

9. The current laws do not grant men even the most basic protection, namely that an aggressor keep their distance from them whether they are a man or a woman (a restraining or protection order).

10. 98% of respondents from across India reported having experienced domestic violence more than once. The study included Indian husbands from a range of socioeconomic classes, but the researchers found that the majority of respondents were from the upper middle class and the middle class.

How is Male Abuse measured?

The researchers surveyed 1000 married men between the ages of 21 and 49. It was community-based, cross-sectional, and used multistage random sampling.

Gender-based violence was reported by 52.4% of men in the current research. Males were abused by their wives or intimate partners in 51.5% of 1000 cases, with 10.5% of those assaults occurring within the previous year. Emotional violence against a partner was more common than physical abuse (51.6%) and 6%, respectively. Only one-tenth of the physical assaults were severe. The husband began the physical and mental assault nearly half of the time. There is no gender symmetry in physical violence in India. Lower family income, middle-class education, a nuclear family structure, and an alcoholic perpetrator were all risk factors. Two way physical aggressions is more common if the earning spouse has completed a graduate degree.

Multiple studies in North America and worldwide have utilized various versions of the Conflict Tactics Scale (CTS) to measure male abuse. The CTS calculates abuse rates based on particular occurrences of both physical and psychological abuse. The 1999 GSS defined numerous categories of psychological or emotional abuse and examined rates of corresponding physical abuse actions, as well as the addition of sexual abuse to physical violence assessment.

Researchers can determine rates of

a. Minor and severe abuse,
b. Each of the specific abusive acts,

c. Overall abuse for a given period prior to the survey using data based on these measures. Respondents are questioned about how frequently they committed or endured any of these acts over a specific time period in order to measure the frequency of abuse.

Reasons for Domestic Violence against Men:
Men frequently cover up the violence they experience at the hands of their spouses or other close relationships for a variety of reasons. Here are some few reasons are as follows:

- Gender stereotypes and facts in society:

As a result of their fear of being judged and labelled as wimpy and effeminate, men frequently experience discrimination or are uncomfortable speaking up about the violence they experience. Because of the gender-specific laws and provisions included in the Indian Constitution, they believe their fight against violence will be in vain. They believe that by not providing for their families, they have failed in their protector role.

- Family pressure and emotional stress:

Even after getting married, the majority of Indians stay in their families' homes. Men are embarrassed to talk about the violence because of this factor.

Additionally, the society has a significant impact on the development of stereotypes and laws that are biased against one gender over another.

- Unemployment and money problems:

Poor financial circumstances, such as not having enough money in their accounts, could enrage a person's wife or partner. The lack of money, which makes it impossible to even meet basic needs, is one of the reasons why women commit domestic violence against men. Additionally, the high unemployment rates among men have been noted over the past few months. As a result, many men have lost their secure jobs and have been able to find new ones. This leads to mental instability and impairs the person's ability to think clearly. Therefore, a person who is unresponsive in the normal course of a household will undoubtedly be creating situations that lead to domestic violence.

- Reasons for Underreporting from a Social and Legal Perspective:

Men who feel that being beaten by a woman is shameful in a society where men predominate tend to keep the violence to themselves and don't report it. In addition, they are unwilling to file any legal claims due to pressure from their families and a fear of falling victim to 498A false accusations. Men who report domestic violence and abuse are frequently not believed by others. Moreover, no one takes these men seriously when they attempt to voice their complaints about the issues in marriage and families. The fact that their wives beat them is something that many men are embarrassed to admit and discuss.

The belief and hope that things would get better, the fear of losing social standing and respect, the need for protection, the love of their families and children, and the fear of being held accountable are among the likely causes of underreporting. In Indian society, where men predominate, complaining by men can also be seen as "feminine behaviour."

Effects of Domestic Violence against Men:

In particular, when violence is experienced at home or by a partner, men are less likely to report violence that is directed at them. Multiple social and cultural norms that encourage violence exist (of all forms). Although most of these norms discriminate against women, increasing the rates and frequency of violence against them, some of them also apply to violence against men, and they are as follows:

1. The topic of intimate partner violence is socially unacceptable, and disclosing abuse is disrespectful.
2. Sexuality and sex are socially unacceptable topics.
3. Conflict resolution through violence is acceptable.
4. People from various social groups, such as homosexuals, are not tolerated in society.
5. Individuals are demotivated from seeking assistance because mental health issues are embarrassing and shameful.

Male domination social standards have created a number of challenges for men as well, which they are effected by in some of the following ways:

1. Men must provide for the household financially because they are the only ones required to work.
2. Men are never taught emotional vulnerability, which causes them to categorise their emotions and has an impact on their mental health.
3. Men are not taught to express their emotions because they are constantly taught to be "strong" and "not sissy."
4. Men are judged negatively for being emotional and sensitive because these are feminine characteristics.
5. Men are never taught how to deal effectively with failure or rejection.
6. If one is not the person in charge of making decisions in their home, they are not a man enough.
7. Additionally, male domination teachings have led to far-reaching conflicts and misrepresented ideas about how men should treat women.
8. There is shame attached to being homosexual.
9. Men are constantly expected to "man up," even if doing so puts their wellbeing and the wellbeing of others at risk.

10. If one does not verbally or physically abuse another person, they are not being a man enough.

Legal Problems- No law to protect men has yet been created by the legislature, despite the data that is available suggesting that there is violence against men. Women are victims of domestic violence under every domestic violence law. The Dowry Prohibition Act of 1961 and the subsequent Section 498A, both of which were enacted by the Supreme Court of India, express concern and the need for the Parliament to enact the necessary changes in order to stop "Legal Terrorism" in the form of the misuse of 498A.

Other Female-Favorable Laws-Man is held responsible for adultery. There is no legal framework in place for a man to file a grievance against his wife or in-laws. The majority of the time, the woman actually files a false 498A complaint against him. Women are treated more kindly and are seen as victims when it comes to divorce and child custody laws. The same is true in regards to post-divorce maintenance. False accusations of rape and sexual harassment against men are becoming more common.

Need Now for Gender Neutral Law:
Gender-neutral laws refer to legislation that treats all people equally without favouring one gender over another. In India, sexual violence laws are primarily aimed at women in order to combat unequal treatment and atrocities against them. These laws ignore the plight of men and members of the transgender community. Stalking, voyeurism, and sexual harassment are examples of gender-specific laws in India. Acid attack is an example of gender-neutral law in Indian law. The following countries have gender-neutral rape laws: the United States, the United Kingdom, Canada, the Philippines, Finland, Ireland, and Australia. Some countries acknowledge both men and women as perpetrators and victims.

Domestic violence laws in India only protect women; they do not protect men. It creates the false impression that men are only capable of being the perpetrator and never the victim. The incidence of domestic violence against men is rising rapidly. Therefore, special clauses and amendments are needed to create gender-neutral laws that will aid victims in obtaining redress and a sentence for the offender regardless of gender. In order to protect both spouses from domestic violence, which is still a problem in our society, specific laws and amendments are required.

Constitutional Provisions:

- **Article 14**: A person's right to equal treatment under the law and protection from it cannot be denied by the state while they are on Indian Territory.
- **Article 15**:Discrimination on the basis of religion, race, caste, sex, or place of birth is prohibited.

Need of the Gender Neutral Law:

We are all aware of our legal system; despite having data on violence against males, there is no act to offer justice for them; in fact, no law has yet been created by law makers to protect men. Laws meant to prevent or control domestic violence regard women as victims. According to Section 498A of the Anti-dowry Laws Prohibition Act of 1961, only males will be made responsible for cruelty to their wives. There is no paragraph or provision that holds women accountable for domestic abuse or protects men from domestic violence in society. Even if males try to open up or disclose their feelings about violence, hardly one listens or takes them seriously because of stereotypes.

Human rights and gender equality, as we are all aware, belong to both men and women in society. Gender-neutral rules, however, are urgently needed in the modern period where males are wrongfully accused of false rape cases, harassment claims, dowry claims, and domestic violence allegations. A woman is treated more kindly and is seen as a victim when it comes to divorce or child custody rules. The same facts are discovered in regards to the request for support following divorce. All of the aforementioned have led to an increase in men being the target of false accusations. Therefore, it is necessary to have rules that are neither gender-biased nor gender-specific.It indicates the presence of domestic violence or any other crime, which should be free of gender bias. Domestic abuse must be treated equally as spousal abuse and cannot be classified according to gender.

Conclusion:

The family structure and society are changing, as are the conventions and ideals surrounding gender violence. Men are also subjected to physical and mental harassment by their husbands and in-laws. As a result, their concerns must be accepted as a social and public health issue, with appropriate measures and solutions addressed. They, too, require assistance in times of stress and domestic violence, particularly by a spouse. Domestic abuse against men must be made a penal offence under the law. Men and women are the foundations of society and families. As a result, laws are required to protect both parties from marital violence.

IV

The emerging legal challenges of defamation in the virtual world: a critical study. [Author: Prachi Gupta]

A speedy and modest technique for sending message, voice, or pictures across worldwide lines is the Internet. At the end of the day, a wellspring of data without limitations on governmental issues or topic, just obliged by the degree of transparency with which the data makers are prepared to share the consequences of their own composition and study. Today, there are a plenty of sites that give data of different sorts. Web access Providers (ISPs) or, once in a while, the organization's IT office make and regulate these sites. These sites are reachable through fitting web search tools, which will find and present data in view of the searcher's requirements.

The reason for the article or piece of examination in this setting is to illuminate the perusers about the reality regarding Cyber Defamation (cybercrime), its predominance in India, different arrangements of the Information Technology Act, and, clearly, extensive answers for assist with keeping this gamble from demonizing individuals and associations.

While the term "cyber defamation" is relatively new, the classic meaning of defamation still holds: any action that damages another's reputation by sign, symbol, or word is considered defamatory. It must be a comment about the plaintiff with the goal to smear their good name. Cyber defamation, on the other hand, entails slandering a person in a novel and far more powerful way, including via the use of advanced electronic tools. Several new legal difficulties have arisen as a result of our more reliant usage of online social networking services. If a defamatory comment appears on a website, blog, or media outlet like a newspaper or magazine, it might be difficult to determine who made the statement and whether or not they meant to damage our reputation. This is because blog writers may be open about their identities or opt to remain anonymous.

"Accordingly, if the claim appears on someone's blog, it may be quite difficult to ascertain the identity of the original author. Since most blogs and news sites do not insist that commenter use their actual names or offer any identifying information (such as their location or email address)," it is very difficult to track down the individuals who read and comment on these pieces. Unfortunately, even if they do, information provided by respondents may be inaccurate. So, keeping tabs on them becomes a herculean task. When someone makes a false and damaging comment about another person and posts it on a social networking site like Facebook, the message immediately becomes viral and is viewed by many people.

This research work tries to bridge the gap between actual happenings of cyber defamation and its awareness in India as well across the globe. It also deals with relevant provisions associated with IT Act and IPC, 1860. This research paper aims to give an in-depth analysis to the readers about the causes and problems related to the abundant cases of cyber-defamation. The lack of awareness regarding issues of cyber sovereignty as a whole is also dealt with effectively in this research work. The probable solutions, findings and suggestions have been included to bridge the gap between vision and actual implementation of the measures.

MEANING AND NATURE OF CYBER DEFAMATION

"Any purposeful bogus correspondence, either composed or spoken, that hurts an individual's standing; diminishes the regard, respect or trust where an individual is held; or incites deriding, unfriendly or unpalatable suppositions or sentiments against an individual is known as defamation."[1]

However, very few businesses are aware of the dangers associated with hosting a website. Who would be responsible, for instance, if a worker secretly posted offensive, chauvinistic, or racial remarks about a competitor on the company's real website? It should be kept in mind that the web differs from other media in a variety of ways. Maligning policies are currently being investigated to depict their likely evolution and potential execution in the internet due to these characteristics. The high level of intelligence seen on the web is one of its key characteristics. Web users have a false sense of informational opportunity thanks to how easily they may get material and communicate with one another. The availability of information on the web is another feature that sets it apart from traditional print or broadcast media. The potential for criticism has clearly increased due to the comparably low cost of online affiliation and, in any case, creating one's own website. Nowadays, anyone can spread content online and face legal action for doing so.

RELEVANCE OF THIS TOPIC IN PRESENT CONTEXT

"The way that users of the web can send messages and post posts on message sheets without unveiling their actual characters is one more significant part of the web. users have the choice of imparting and posting utilizing made up names or secretly." [2]

Users are now much less careful about the content of their messages as a result of this factor, which makes the internet more prone to defamation. Additionally, it improves one's ability to access the internet from the privacy and security of their own home or place of business and the responsive, logical design of online communications. Slander is the willful violation of another person's absolute right to privacy and good name. The unjustly and purposefully disseminated remarks or activities that are coordinated against a person can harm that person's status, good name, or notoriety in the public eye.

Slander is written maligning, whereas criticism is spoken maligning. "Just when misleading cases are aimed at somebody other than the objective may an individual's standing be hurt; as such, the disparaging explanation should be unveiled to fulfill the distribution prerequisite."[3]

EXPLANATION OF CYBER CRIME AND ITS DIMENSIONS

The term "web" refers to a really broad concept that includes more than just the internet and also includes PCs as a vital type of media used to access networks, data, programming, and other things. Cybercrime is defined as any infringement involving a computer or the use of a PC network. Censuring behaviour can be categorised into two groups: offensive and hostile behaviour. Analysis defame implies the displaying of injuring an individual or association's name and repute through verbally communicated phrases or opinions, however analysis insult alludes to accomplishing as such using produced articulations. Its certificate integrates unapproved access, unapproved catch endeavors, data adjusting, infringement including young person suggestive amusement, stupid use of development, etc.

Everybody has the choice to one side to talk openly of discourse and explanation, as indicated by the Constitution's Article 19(1) (a) on Freedom of Speech and Expression. Such opportunity is believed to be dependent upon conceivable requirements. A word or remark that sabotages someone else's standing could expose the speaker to lawful results under the censuring rule. The affirmation of someone else's standing falls under the domain of sensible constraint. "The earliest iteration of the term "cybercrime" solely included the theft or destruction of computer programs and data. However, incidences of character slander, unlawful access to pornography, illegal gambling, and online stalking are now regarded as serious crimes."[4]

JUDICIAL PRONOUNCEMENTS ON CYBER DEFAMATION

"In the first case discussed here, the applicant in Kalandi Charan Lenka v. Territory of Odisha was the objective of web following, and a fake record was made in her name. Also, the guilty party sent revolting messages to the companions with an end goal to dishonor the applicant."[5]

What's more, it decided that the litigant is denied from making bogus or libelous charges recorded as a hard copy or individual. A notable saying from the Spiderman stories, "With incredible power comes huge obligation," impeccably summarizes the utilization of innovation and its true capacity for misuse.

Correspondence has been considerably more helpful since the web period started. However, there is an expense for such comfort. Because of how easily information and data can be transferred on the web, it has become a big target for criticism. Despite the fact that there are laws in existence that ban distributing slanderous information over the internet, the vast majority of individuals are either oblivious to these prohibitions or are behaving much too irresponsibly.

The widespread usage of online entertainment sparked a revolution in India as well as other parts of the world. The extraordinary growth of the Internet has given people a platform to share their thoughts, feelings, and opinions through many channels. However, there are concerns since anonymous Internet users may exploit these technical platforms in the name of free speech and expression, and this is a consequence of the ease with which information can be accessed and shared online. Accordingly, "Digital Defamation" has occurred on a small scale. Slander, in its classic sense, is the damaging of a person's reputation in the eyes of a third party, and it may be done by verbal or written communication, as well as signals and apparent depictions, which includes digital maligning. The claim should make reference to the offended party, and the intention should be to defame the person against whom the claim has been made.

"However, cyber-maligning involves criticizing a person using a fresh and unquestionably more effective tactic, such as the use of modern electronic devices. It refers to the dissemination of negative information about somebody online or with the aid of PCs or the Internet. The distribution of any kind of defamatory statements about another person on a website or the sending of E-mails to that person that contain defamatory information would be considered defamatory statements and would be subject to cyber criticism."

"PROBLEMS AND ISSUES IN CYBER DEFAMATION"

Our nation's steadily increasing reliance on the Internet for long-distance interpersonal connection has given rise to a number of real problems. Finding the person who intended to damage our reputation or the outsider who read the defamatory statement can be the toughest challenge in a defamation lawsuit, especially when it comes to websites or other media outlets like newspapers or magazines.

This is due to the fact that bloggers may decide to protect their anonymity or maintain their candour. "Accordingly, in the event that the assertion shows up on somebody's blog, recognizing the author may be troublesome. Since most sites don't expect users to utilize their genuine personalities or give any crucial data, like name, area, or email address, considerably harder to recognize the perusers leave remarks on websites or online reports."[6] Regardless of whether they, someone could still provide false information. Therefore, locating these people is challenging. "When a defamatory statement is posted online, especially on virtual entertainment platforms like Facebook, it travels quickly and is read by many people, which hurts the person who made the statement."

CRITICAL ANALYSIS OF LAW

Differentiating computerized guidelines and techniques in India and the UK reveals a couple of likenesses in unambiguous locales and differences in others. Most assortments can be made through different ways. Regardless, India over the span of late years has exceptionally raised base on network security as need might arise, despite a noteworthy irrefutable permission to development and resource shortage. "Conversely, with India, the UK has more developed systems and cycles, and organization wellbeing has in like manner been a worry for policymakers for a more long time period. Conversely, with India, the UK has a more generous organization insurance designing. In any case, neither India nor the UK can apply existing standards to new circumstances in the internet."[7]

Furthermore, the UK is significantly more open to partner input while forming its arrangements than India is, where both private and public undertakings will generally focus on issues of public safety. "For this situation, the Indian government can do a ton to bring issues to light about network protection and can likewise utilize the versatile techniques utilized by the UK with comply to security best practices without essentially requiring extreme regulations and guidelines."[8] It ought to in like manner explore the chance of shutting tranquil agreements that give the level of participation essential for analyzing cyberthreats. The UK ought to sort out some sort of concordance between its worries about open wellbeing and those about normal opportunities associated with security and perception. "Via online entertainment, individuals pitch their commitment, separations, and pregnancy news.

Via online entertainment, a significant number of us are becoming public with our relationship situations with, perspectives, our confirmations of mistakes, and our sexual directions." [9] With the recently referenced models, web defaming and savaging influence chance of explanation in the short-and long stretch. Web based goading and defamation can have negative mental and significant effects as well as money related, legitimacy, and various results. Bots have actually been misusing development by leaving comments and responses. A wide range of cybercrimes, electronic trade, chance of enunciation, authorized development opportunities, legitimate inquiries, and insurance honors are completely covered under cyberlaw. "Visa distortion, unapproved permission to PC systems, adolescent sexual diversion, programming and gear burglary, and advanced following are cases of cybercrimes. Regardless of the way that oversight, obscenity guidelines, and analysis fall inside the umbrella of chance of articulation."[10]

The earliest accentuation of the saying "cybercrime" solely covered the thievery or decimation of PC tasks and data. In any case, paces of character criticize, unlawful permission to sexual diversion, unlawful wagering, and electronic following are at present seen as serious infringement. "Online amusement is used to report responsibility, partitions, and pregnancy announcements. Countless us moreover use it to articulate our relationship circumstances with, our thoughts, surrender our issues, and declare our sexual bearing, which was amazing ten years prior."[11] As per the previously mentioned assertions, web based savaging and criticism affect opportunity of articulation both right away and after some time. Online provocation and maligning can have negative mental and substantial impacts as well as monetary, validity, and different results. Bots have as of late been manhandling innovation by leaving remarks and reactions.

CONCLUSION

There is an urgent need for a framework that informs and enlightens people about what is appropriate and unsightly, off-base and right, and slanderous and non-disparaging conduct on the internet. The mediators who provide such an open forum should also be aware of the content placed there and take decisive action against those who submit such derogatory material in order to prevent repetition in the future. With the development of the advanced era, both the application of innovation and its potential abuse have become non-comprehensive topics. The simplicity of communication has substantially advanced. However, such ease comes at a price. Because of how easily information and data can be transferred, slander is one of the most well-known cybercrimes. Many individuals are either too careless to realize the difference between defamatory and non-defamatory information or are ignorant of the rules that prohibit the sharing of such stuff online.

SUGGESTIONS

Having an independent computerized criminal assessment cell that reports to the Central Bureau of Investigation is supported. "This cell ought to be spread out independently so it reports to the central government and is committed to looking at computerized infringement, for instance, advanced analysis. To help them with overseeing evildoers quickly, every region in each locale of India should have a computerized cell police base camp drove by an assessment official who is capable on computerized regulations."[12] The public authority should start care missions to show general society cybercrimes and the security steps they should take.

Legitimate chief can moreover expect a basic part in the event that exceptional computerized courts are spread out and chosen with explicit specific data could coordinate these courts. Along these lines, there is a need to plan legitimate authorities, police work power to settle cases of computerized bad behavior rapidly and even more. "Information and correspondence development proceeds to change, and people need to get invigorated with its new development. So we need to address existing guidelines to keep awake with advancement and hinder such offenses happening and affecting people at large."[13]

[1] Gunjan, V.K., Kumar, A. and Avdhanam, S., 2013, September. A survey of cyber crime in India. In 2013 15th international conference on advanced computing technologies (ICACT) (pp. 1-6). IEEE.

[2] Stone, A. and Williams, G., 2000. Freedom of Speech and Defamation: Developments in the Common Law World. Monash UL Rev., 26, p.362

[3] Ibid

[4] Sarmah, A., Sarmah, R. and Baruah, A.J., 2017. A brief study on Cyber Crime and Cyber Law's of India. International Research

Journal of Engineering and Technology (IRJET), 4(6), pp.1633-1640.

[5] Valdaya, A., 2014. Legal Consequences of Online Defamation in India. Available at SSRN 2386983.

[6] Little, L.E., 2012. Internet defamation, freedom of expression, and the lessons of private international law for the United States. European Yearbook of Private International Law, 14, pp.2013-03.

[7] Halder, D. furthermore, Jaishankar, K., 2016. Digital violations against ladies in India. SAGE Publications India

[8] Kashyap, A., 2016. DEFAMATION IN INTERNET AGE: LAW & ISSUES IN INDIA. International Journal for Innovations in Engineering, Management and Technology, 1(1), pp.17-25.

[9] Ibid

[10] Chhetri, S., 2021. The Defamation in the Internet Age: Cyber Defamation. Issue 1 Int'l JL Mgmt. and Human., 4, p.1981.

[11] Stone, A. furthermore, Williams, G., 2000. The right to speak freely of Speech and Defamation: Developments in the Common Law World. Monash UL Rev., 26, p.362

[12] Knox-Mawer, R., 1956. Criticism: Some Indian Precedents and the Common Law. Global and Comparative Law Quarterly, 5(2), pp.282-285.

[13] Little, L.E., 2012. Web maligning, opportunity of articulation, and the examples of private global regulation for the United States. European Yearbook of Private International Law, 14, pp.2013-03.

V

12 Universal Laws for leading a Blissful Life. [Author: Manju Kumari]

To begin with, the term "Universe" is derived from two words. Firstly, Uni- means "one" and secondly, verse-means "writing arranged in lines which have a definite rhythm and often finish with the same sound (rhyme)". Therefore, to summarise the term Universe is defined as everything that exists in the whole space is created from the one source. From a spiritual perspective, the Universe is just another name for a higher power that exists which we call Supreme God. That the universe is wholly ruled by the Universal laws which helps to fulfil the purpose for the whole existence.

Everything is Energy?

Of course, is it true that Everything is Energy and Energy is Everything. The German dramatist and thinker Gotthold Lessing observed that -"In nature everything is connected, everything is interwoven, everything changes with everything, everything merges from one into another."

· *Body = Intelligence = Mind = Information = Energy = Consciousness = Spirit = Supreme God. The human body, plant and all physical things are made up of matter and energy. It's all the same thing. It's all ONE thing and everything is energy.*

For example: If we observe our body and start looking down from skin to organs, organs to tissues, tissues to cells, cells to molecules and molecules to atoms then deep down we just feel a divine energy which is connected to everything around and all living organisms constantly take in and release energy.

The Spiritual concept of Energy, Vibration and Frequency

Energy is the source; Vibration is the movement and Frequency is the number of vibrations created by movement. That the whole existence is the manifestation of single thought, and it continuously manifests due to continuous vibrations of the energy. As all things in our universe are constantly in motion and vibrating.

"If you want to find the secrets of the universe, think in terms of energy, frequency and vibration." – Nikola Tesla

Besides the basic concept of vibrational frequency, the spiritual phenomenon is also defined as our body is made of molecules, which are vibrating constantly, and creating electromagnetic energy waves.

"Everything is energy. And that's all there is to it. Match the frequency of the reality you want, and you cannot help but get that reality. It can be no other way. This is not philosophy. This is physics."
– Albert Einstein.

Whereas, when Einstein talks about matching the frequency he means that everything we desire has a frequency set point. We don't think about it in those terms but all beings – all things in the universe – vibrate at a certain level.

Further, Vibrational energy experts claim that certain emotions and thought patterns, such as joy, peace, and acceptance, create high frequency vibrations, while other feelings and mindsets (such as anger, despair, and fear) vibrate at a lower rate.

As a result, the creation is nothing more than the energy manifesting itself in various ways throughout the entire cosmos. because we are all related and have a single awareness. If we start looking inside by way of meditation or start observing nature, then we will find that things inside and outside are co-dependent and connected deep down.

What is Naad?

The Naad is called the eternal sound of the universe. The primary characteristic of the sound is the vibration and movement. Every action responds to the sound creating vibration and movement. Therefore, everything at physical level is the result of vibration and movement. The vibration thought to have started with the universe's creation and has been resonating through our very being ever since is called Naad. In fact, it connects with the time when we start to find ourselves as well as the awakening of our kundalini and spiritual development.

What is the Universal Sound?

Om is a sacred 'mantra'. It is considered the seed of all universal sounds and words. According to the Big Bang theory, Om is the cosmic sound that initiated the creation of the universe. Further, in Hindu scripture, it is defined as the foundational sound of creation.

Recently, NASA has released the sound from a black hole from which it also came to know that OM (AUM) is the sound of the Universe. New NASA Black Hole Sonifications with a Remix | NASA

For example: When we chant **OM (AUM)** consciously the body starts vibrating at the frequency of 432Hz, which is the same vibrational frequency of everything in nature. As such, AUM is the basic sound of the universe, so by chanting it, we are symbolically and physically acknowledging our connection to nature and all other living beings.

Hence, OM sound is considered as the Original Sound of the Universe.

What is the Source of Universal Laws?

The Source is the origin of the 12 universal rules (also known as God, the Universe, Higher Power, etc.). These universal rules were not created by humans; rather, just like physical laws like the law of gravity, they were discovered by them via their observations and experiences. The spiritual science is also known as metaphysics. Metaphysics is the area of philosophy that deals with the nature of existence, truth and knowledge.

The following verse is from **chapter 10 of the Bhagavad Gita,** in which Lord Krishna, said that "There is no possibility of anything in the universe—a sun, a star, or you and me—existing separately". To me, this unifying force is the infinite love of the Lord, operating on the physical level. Just as all of us are one, so all things in the created universe are one in the Lord.**Bhagavad Gita – Wikipedia**

What are the 12 universal laws?

The 12 universal laws are believed to be inherent, immutable principles of our universe that prehistoric peoples have always intuitively understood. Beyond the purview of human-made rules, metaphysical laws (sometimes referred to as spiritual laws) give us directives for living (body-mind-spirit). That's right that the 12 universal laws are unchangeable and getting familiar with each universal law can help us to unlock a more spiritually aligned life which helps to master life on all levels and gives us insights into what we can do to reach our goals. The universal laws are following:

1. LAW OF DIVINE ONENESS- Everything is connected. To understand this law is to be more compassionate towards others. We all have the same ability to make mistakes; and the same ability to achieve greatness.

2. LAW OF VIBRATION- Everything is in constant motion. The people we meet and the objects we hold, are all vibrating at their own frequency, and we must match the energy of the things we desire in order to obtain them.

3. LAW OF CORRESPONDENCE- Our lives are created by our daily, subconscious patterns. In order to change, we must first identify the thoughts and habits that are holding us back.

4. LAW OF ATTRACTION- What like unto itself is drawn. To put it simply: focus on the things you want and not the things you do not want. Truly believe you are capable of having what you want, and the universe will present it to you.

5. LAW OF ACTION- As above, so below. Listen to your inner guidance. As stated above, the law of attraction will present you with endless opportunities, but it is up to you to take the necessary steps to attain what you've asked for.

6. LAW OF CAUSE & EFFECT- Manifestation requires aligned actions. Also known as karma. Probably the most straightforward law; whatever you give in this life -good or bad- you will get in return.

7. LAW OF COMPENSATION- Every action has a consequence. Your efforts will never go unnoticed. Trust that the universe wants to reward you and be open to its limitless forms of compensation. We are awarded for the right action.

8. LAW OF PERPETUAL TRANSMUTATION OF ENERGY- Situations occur that give low vibrational frequencies and bring on emotions such as anger and sadness: both which are valid emotions and should be felt in their entirety. However, there comes a time when you need to tap into your power and get yourself back to a positive frequency. Energy is always moving and always changing.

9. LAW OF RELATIVITY- Just because we are all connected does not mean we all live the same physical reality. Yet still, no situation is good nor bad until it is put up for comparison. It is best to keep our perspectives neutral and learn to be grateful without having the need to compare. It's all relative.

10. LAW OF POLARITY- There are two sides to everything. Everything has an opposite, and learning is part of the human experience. Take what did not work in a previous situation, and apply new, opposing methods in your next venture.

11. LAW OF RHYTHM- Nothing is permanent. Life is a never-ending cycle. It is important to embrace every moment and to remember not to stretch the natural order of things.

12. LAW OF GENDER- Manifestation requires a balance of energy. We are made up of two major types of energy, which are thought about easiest as masculine and feminine. Allow room for both energies and find a balance that suits you best.

The 12 spiritual principles of the cosmos are meant to guide us as we harmonize our surroundings to bring about better realities while pursuing pleasure via love and forgiveness. Further, to achieve true pleasure and appreciate our purpose in the cosmos we require to understand and put these 12 fundamental laws into practice. For more clarity and understanding these 12 universal laws are further divided in 21 subcategories.

The 21 Universalsub-lawsAare:

1. Aspiration to a Higher Power
2. Charity
3. Compassion
4. Courage
5. Dedication/ Devotion
6. Faith
7. Forgiveness
8. Generosity
9. Grace
10. Honesty
11. Hope
12. Joy
13. Kindness
14. Leadership
15. Non interference
16. Patience
17. Praise
18. Responsibility
19. Self love
20. Thankfulness
21. Unconditional love

To summarize the whole content, it is stated that all these **33 universal spiritual laws** are applicable to both physical and non-physical phenomena. It is thought that these laws have existed since the dawn of time and control the spiritual health of everyone in this cosmos. These are universal rules which help to live a blissful and peaceful life. In addition, attaining eternal bliss and happiness is only the soul purpose of this journey.

The laws are not intended to constrain our thinking, but to broaden it in a way that fosters a genuine awareness and connection to others as well as to oneself.

"Energy is the Currency of the Universe. The universe's secrets are encoded in your cells;thus, you already own all the knowledge you will ever need. The Light Will Set You Free."

If you feel, as we do, that this knowledge should be available to all, please share this on social media, email to a friend, or talk about it with loved ones. You'll not just be helping them; you'll be helping us all, the entire Collective Consciousness. Articles for all 12 Universal Laws and other spiritual content is to be available on the website. Enjoy them all and let them lead you to a higher understanding and a better quality of life!

Make full use of your ability to inspire, motivate, or excite the one you love now!

VI

The urgency to reform the Juvenile Justice system and not the juvenile: An attempt to change. [Author: Muskan Mittal]

The legal age of adulting as per law is 18 years of age. However, due to societal changes, the current generation is maturing at a very young age, which leads us to a very pertinent question. Are they mature enough to face the consequences?[1]Children in criminal justice procedures have traditionally been treated similarly to adults and subjected to the same criminal justice processes as adults. Children in Australia were subjected to the same punishments as adults until the early twentieth century, including hard labour, corporal and capital punishment (Carrington & Pereira 2009).

Section **2(33)** of the JJ Act, 2015 states *"heinous offences" includes the offences for which the minimum punishment under the Indian Penal Code (45 of 1860) or any other law for the time being in force is imprisonment for seven years or more.*[2]

Section **2(54)** of the JJ Act, 2015 states *"serious offences" includes the offences for which the punishment under the Indian Penal Code (45 of 1860) or any other law for the time being in force, is imprisonment between three to seven years.*[3]

In India, every time a juvenile commits any crime whether petty, serious or a heinous one, an attempt is made to reform him instead of punishing to save his future and life ahead. This offender centric approach in the country has resulted in injustice to the victims of many heinous offences. It's high time to punish the heinous offenders whether child or adult and to ensure the real justice to victims.

INADEQUACY OF THE CURRENT LEGISLATIONS

Juvenile Justice Act made on lines of Indian Penal Code which is a pre-constitutional law made by britishers on the basis of circumstances prevailing at that time.[4] The act although amended in 2015 has been ineffective in reforming juvenile delinquents and reducing crime rate among children. Therefore, now is the high time to amend it again and create a deterrence in the mind of children about the consequences of committing offences, predominantly the heinous one.

The horrific Nirbhaya Case being wrongly interpreted and legislated

In the Nirbhaya Case,[5] in December 2012, a paramedical student was gang-raped and killed in New Delhi. One of the defendants in this matter was 17-year old when the crime was committed. As a result of the juvenile laws in place at the time, the adolescent received less harsh penalty than other rapists as other rapists were sentenced to death.

He was the fifth person to be charged with gang rape and the murder of a 23-year-old woman. The Juvenile Justice Board's report contained no proof that he was the most vicious perpetrator of the incident. As a result, after three years in the reformation home, he was released.

The juvenile's case was the most contentious because of the horrific crime he did and the sentence he received under the Indian legal system. As a result, people demanded that the juvenile rapist be treated as an adult in the case because it was such a horrific act.

Intelligence agents suspected the adolescent of becoming radicalised in 2015 since he shared a cell with another adolescent who was implicated in the Delhi High Court bombing. As a result, when investigating the case of this adolescent implicated in a gang rape in Delhi, intelligence officials kept this in mind.

In November 2015, a month before his release, Nirbhaya's family sought that the juvenile's identity be made public, but his identity was never revealed, and he was freed despite widespread public criticism.So, in the Nirbhaya case, which is regarded as India's most heinous rape, the judiciary operated in this manner.

The tremendous outrage resulted in modifications to the legislation governing children who break the law in 2015. After that, the Lok Sabha passed the Juvenile Justice (Care and Protection of Children) Act, which stated that children aged 16 to 18 might be treated as adults if they[6] were suspected of committing serious crimes.

This incident clearly draws a line between heinous offenders of different age groups doing the same offence. The act which the legislature after such deep driver thought and research have made is not only inadequate but also unfortunate for the victim and victim's family such as in the "Mercedes Hit and Run Case."[7]

Sunil (Juvenile) v. State of M.P.[8]

In this case, a Criminal Revision was filed by the petitioner under Section 102 of the Juvenile Justice (Care and Protection of Children) Act, 2015. The allegation against the petitioner was that he is aged around 15 years old and on 16-01-2021 he had committed rape of a minor girl aged around 10-11 years old.

The Court while dismissing the petition observed that,[9] "The Legislature has still not learnt any lesson from the case[10]as the age of a child is still kept below 16 years in heinous offences under section15 of the Act of 2015 giving a free hand to the delinquents under the age of 16 years to commit heinous offences. Thus, apparently, despite committing a heinous offence, the petitioner would be tried as a juvenile only, because he is less than 16 years old as provided under Section 15 of Act of 2015. Apparently, the present law to deal with such cases is totally inadequate and ill equipped and this Court really wonders as to how many more Nirbhaya's sacrifice would be required to shake the conscious of the lawmakers of this Country."[11]

LEGISLATURE BEING STUBBORN INSPITE MANY ATTEMPTS

The Parliamentary Standing Committee on Home Affairs, headed by Congress MP Anand Sharma, in its report submitted to Rajya Sabha observed that there has been a large number of cases under the Protection of Children from Sexual Offences (POCSO) Act where the age of juvenile offenders has been below the threshold age for applicability of the law.

The committee said that it believed that minor sexual offenders may commit more serious and heinous crime if left untreated and uncounselled. Therefore, it is very important to re-look at[12] these provisions "because more and more juveniles are getting involved in such crimes", the report stated.

"The committee, therefore, recommends that the MHA may take up with MoW&CD (Ministry of Women and Child Development) to review the current age limit of 18 years and see if it can be reduced to 16 years for the applicability of the POCSO Act, 2012," the report said.[13]

The same can be rightly applied to the Juvenile Justice Act as well. The present law strictly drawing a line between adult offenders and the juvenile offenders of the same crime is misused more than being helpful. The object for the Juvenile Justice Act which was to save the future of these delinquents is in reality non-sensical and contrary to the interest of other people of society which expects law to be a saviour and not an excuse.

WHY THIS SUBJECT IS A NEED OF THE HOUR?

A primary principle underlying the juvenile court since its inception more than a century ago has been that juvenile criminals should not be prosecuted in adult criminal courts. Juvenile court was established to deal with juvenile criminals based on their age rather than their crimes. Instead of punishment, the goal of juvenile court is to provide treatment, reformation and assistance. During the 1980s and 1990s, the public demanded that juveniles be treated harshly and tried as adults. Many states have implemented laws making it easier to try some juvenile criminals as adults, and some have even proposed abolishing juvenile courts. Those juveniles who in their absolute mental capacity commit heinous crimes must not be tried in the juvenile courts but the adult courts because:

1. Their objective is to protect minors from the consequences of their own conduct, which is based on faulty premises.

2. The juvenile court is ineffective in preventing juvenile violence.

3. To prevent the next generation from becoming predators, we must punish juvenile criminals in order to address the current juvenile crime problem.

4. Justice mandates that juvenile courts be abolished (for certain class of juvenile)—juveniles will be allowed their entire range of constitutional rights if they are tried in adult courts.[14]

Therefore, we are already running late in understanding the negative impact and the consequences of the current juvenile legislative system and it is high time to re-think and re-legislate on this subject.

WHY NOT REFORM BUT PUNISH?

These juvenile offenders shall be punished:

- Because punishing juveniles committing heinous crimes instead of sparing them will act as measure of deterrence to forbid any such future acts.

- These juveniles who commit or involve in such heinous acts are aware of right and wrong.
- Therefore, the actions are the result of their choice of wrong path and not lack of understanding.
- Instead of rehabilitation, they should be tried as adults and punished in order to prevent other minors from committing such heinous deeds.
- Juveniles are also capable of influencing other children to involve into such terrific activities if not treated rightly.
- The deciding factor for punishment shall be the mental and physical maturity of a child and not his age.

WHICH JUVENILES ARE BEING TALKED ABOUT?

Youths under the age of 18 commit murder, rape, and other horrible crimes every day. What is it about them that makes them deserving of special treatment? According to Section 15 of the JJ Act, the Juvenile Justice Board in the district should consider three factors when determining whether the child should be tried as an adult or as a juvenile, with a maximum sentence of three years in a special home.[15] The criteria are whether the child has the mental and physical capacity to commit the crime, understands the consequences, and the circumstances surrounding the crime. If the Board decides that the child can be tried as an adult, the case is sent to a special juvenile court, which reviews the Board's decision.[16] These criteria mentioned in the law are vague enough to act as a loophole more than the law. The author is talking about the juvenile offenders who just because of being minor under the law i.e., under 18 are spared or given vey less punishment for their dreadful and horrific deeds. *The author is requesting the legislature to reconsider the provisions of juvenile justice act, 2015 and reduce the age of child to 16 yearsi.e., remove the provisions of preliminary assessment in case of heinous offences being committed by people of 16-18 years and to try the juveniles committing such heinous crimes as adults (So that anymore Nirbhaya has to not sacrifice!).*

In Indian criminal system, "essentially, the trial in the regular court is offence-oriented; in the juvenile court, it is offender-oriented. In other words, in the children's court, societal safety and the child's future are balanced. For an adult offender, prison is the default option; for a juvenile it is the last resort".

But when the child is capable enough to understand the consequences and chose to commit that heinous offence which in reality not only affects the victim but devastatingly affects the whole society, why is that person thought for the benefits and is getting spared by law. The juvenile chose to destroy the victim's current and future life giving him/her physical, mental, financial loss as well as the loss of his/her reputation. These juveniles should not be spared in the name of incapacity or non-understanding and must be punished as much as they deserve so as to deter the future offenders and save the young generations from involving in such unlawful activities.

CONCLUSION

It is quite understandable that as a teenager, one is bound to make mistakes. This article is not an attempt to sentence a teenage boy or girl to a year in jail who enters a mall and shoplifts. The whole purpose of this article is to help the people, society and lawmakers understand the present situation and change in trend in juvenile delinquency. Today's generation is mature more than their age to distinguish between right and wrong and the child who in spite knowing the distinction and consequences involved in the wrongful heinous activities must be treated none other than adults. If the punishment is a concern, simply do not commit the offence. This way, children will be deterred from committing terrific crimes and a change can be observed in the increasing crime rate of juvenile offenders. The change requires one more thing i.e., an attempt to create awareness on a large scale by the government and associated institutions including NGOs.

[1]Rohit Singh, *Are Reforms Really Needed in the Juvenile Justice*, LEGAL SERVICE INDIA.COM (Aug. 1, 2022, 5:00 PM), http://www.legalservicesindia.com/article/1689/Are-Reforms-

Really-Needed-in-the-Juvenile-Justice.html.

[2] The Juvenile Justice Act (Care and Protection of Children) Act, 2015, § 2(33), No. 2, Acts of Parliament, 2016 (India).

[3]The Juvenile Justice Act (Care and Protection of Children) Act, 2015, § 2(54), No. 2, Acts of Parliament, 2016 (India).

[4]THE DAILY GUARDIAN, https://thedailyguardian.com/reforming-the-juvenile-justice-system/(last visited Nov. 30, 2022).

[5] Mukesh &Anr v. State for NCT of Delhi &Ors., (2017) 6 SCC 1.

[6] FINANCIAL EXPRESS, https://www.financialexpress.com/india-news/arvind-kejriwals-aap-govt-in-delhi-wants-to-try-boys-above-15-as-adults-for-rape-eyes-death-penalty-too/153736/ (last visited Dec. 31, 2022).

[7] NDTV, https://www.ndtv.com/india-news/serious-not-heinous-rules-supreme-court-in-teens-hit-and-run-case-2161669, (last visited Nov. 30, 2022).

[8] Criminal Revision No.853/2021, decided on 25-06-2021.

[9] SCC ONLINE BLOG, https://www.scconline.com/blog/post/2021/06/29/rape-case/ (last visited Dec. 29, 2022).

[10] Mukesh v. State NCT of Delhi, (2017) 6 SCC 1.

[11]Supra Note 9.

[12] Par panel asks govt to consider reducing juvenile delinquency age to 16 under POCSO Act. (2021, March 16). Metrovaartha.Com; .http://www.english.metrovaartha.com/news/35307/par-panel-asks-govt-to-consider-reducing-juvenile-delinquency-age-to-16-under-pocso-act.

[13]MINT, https://www.livemint.com/news/india/house-panel-recommends-reducing-juvenile-delinquency-age-to-16-under-pocso-act-11615895930083.html(last visited August 2, 2002).

[14]CLIFFS NOTES, https://www.cliffsnotes.com/study-guides/criminal-justice/the-juvenile-justice-system/should-juveniles-be-tried-as-adults(last visited Dec.5, 2022).

[15] THE INDIAN EXPRESS, https://indianexpress.com/article/explained/when-a-juvenile-is-tried-as-an-adult-when-not-5840823/ (last visited Dec.8, 2022).

[16]Ibid.

VII

Electoral Integrity and the Indian Constitution. [Author: Vaishali Yadav]

"I mean to diminish no individual, institution or phase in our history when I say that India is valued the world over for a great many things, but for three over all others : The Taj Mahal; Mahatma Gandhi; and India's electoral democracy."

Electoral integrity refers to international standards and global norms governing the appropriate conduct of elections.

These standards have been endorsed in a series of authoritative conventions, treaties, protocols, and guidelines by agencies of the international community, notably by the decisions of the UN General Assembly, by regional bodies such as the Organization for Security and Cooperation in Europe , the Organization of American States , and the African Union , and by member states in the United Nations. Following endorsement, these standards apply universally to all countries throughout the electoral cycle, including during the pre-electoral period, the campaign, on polling day, and in its aftermath.

India is a sovereign, socialist, secular, democratic republic. Democracy runs like a golden thread in the social, economic and political fabric woven by the Constitution given by 'We, the People of India' unto ourselves. The concept of democracy as visualized by the Constitution pre-supposes the representation of the people in Parliament and State legislatures by the method of election. The Supreme Court has held that democracy is one of the inalienable basic features of the Constitution of India and forms part of its basic structure. The Constitution of India adopted a Parliamentary form of government. Parliament consists of the President of India and the two Houses — Rajya Sabha and Lok Sabha. India, being a Union of states, has separate state legislatures for each state. State legislatures consist of the Governor and two Houses — Legislative Council and Legislative Assembly — in seven states, namely, Andhra Pradesh, Telangana, Bihar, Jammu & Kashmir, Karnataka, Maharashtra and Uttar Pradesh, and of the Governor and the state Legislative Assembly in the remaining 22 states. Apart from the above, two out of the seven Union Territories, namely, National Capital Territory of Delhi and Puducherry, also have their Legislative Assemblies.

After studying this lesson, you will be able to l describe the composition of the Election Commission of India; l enumerate the functions the Election Commission and explain its role; l recall the procedure of election from the announcement of schedule, to the declaration of the result; l mention various stages in the electoral process; l recognize the poll-related officers and describe their functions; l identify the drawbacks and need for electoral reforms; l suggest the electoral reforms and those already carried on.

Tenure and Removal Chief Election Commissioner and other Election Commissioners

They are appointed for a term of six years, or till the age of 65 whichever is earlier. It is important that Chief Election Commissioner and other Election Commissioners should be free from all political interferences. Therefore, even if they are appointed by the President, they cannot be removed by him. And no changes can be brought in the conditions of service and the tenure of office after their appointment. The Chief Election Commissioner cannot be removed from office, except on the grounds and in the manner on which the Supreme Court judges can be removed. However, since the other Election Commissioners and the Regional Election Commissioners work under the Chief Commissioner, they may be removed by the President on his recommendations.

Electoral reforms

In order to restore the confidence of the public in the democratic electoral system, many electoral reforms have been recommended from time to time by Tarkunde Committee and Goswami Committee which were particularly appointed to study and report on the scheme for Electoral Reforms in the year 1974 and 1990 respectively. Out of these recommendations some have been implemented. In fact, it was under the chairmanship of the then Chief Election Commissioner, T.N. Seshan, that Election Commission initiated many more measures to ensure free and fair elections. Some of the reforms which have been implemented so far are as follows:

1. The voting age has been lowered from 21 years to 18 years. This has helped increase the number of voters and response confidence in the youth of the country.

2. Another landmark change has been the increase in the amount of security deposit by the candidate to prevent many non-serious candidates from contesting elections with an ulterior motive. MODULE - 4 Notes 208 Political Science Structure of Government

3. The photo identity cards have been introduced to eradicate bogus voting or impersonation.

4. With the introduction of Electronic Voting Machine (EVM) the voting capturing, rigging, and bogus voting may not be possible. The use of EVM will in the long run result in reducing the cost of holding elections and also the incidence of tampering during counting of votes.

5. If a discrepancy is found between the member of votes polled and number of total votes counted, the Returning officer away report the matter forthwith to Election Commission. Election Commission on such report may either declare the poll at the particular polling station as void and give a date for fresh poll or countermand election in that constituency. There is no doubt that India needs drastic poll reforms but still the fact remains that Indian elections have been largely free and fair and successfully conducted. It gives the country the proud distinction of being the largest democracy in the world.

Election Commission

The Constitution of India has made provisions for all three of these requisites. India has an independent Election Commission which handles and controls the direction and superintendence of the electoral rolls. It also handles the conduct of elections to the offices of the President of India, Vice-President of India, and the elections to State Legislatures. In the event that any situation arises for which the laws that have been enacted by the Parliament have no provision or insufficient provision, the Election Commission is empowered to issue special directions and orders to deal with it.

A body similar to the Election Commission was formed as an independent constitutional authority to conduct elections to local bodies, panchayats and municipalities. Election Commission of India (ECI) Election Commission of India is a permanent Constitutional body established in accordance with the constitution on 25th January 1950. Dr. B.R. Ambedkar expressed the objectives of the Election Commission of India in the following words: "Our country is vast, consisting of different races, languages, cultures, religions, classifications etc. So, the Election Commission consisting of the Chief Election Commissioner for all India level is required to prevent injustice which may otherwise happen to mixed population. This central body works with, free from local influences and shall have the control over the entire election machinery in the country". In Indian constitution Part XV, Articles 324-329 deals election commission of India. Originally the Commission had only a

Chief Election Commissioner, at present it consists of Chief Election Commissioner and two Election Commissioners. For the first time two additional commissioners were appointed on 16th October 1989 but they had a very short tenure till 1st January 1990.

Electoral System in India

An electoral system is a set of rules set for the smooth functioning and conduction of elections. It also decides how their results are determined. Being a sovereign, socialist, secular, democratic republic, Indian government organises political electoral systems.

The rules under the electoral process govern all aspects, including elections, who can vote, candidates, ballots, campaigning and other factors, of the voting process. Defined by constitutions and electoral laws, political electoral systems are typically conducted by election commissions.

The number of winners elected vary in different types of elections. Like for a unique position like that of prime minister, president or governor, electoral systems elect a single winner; and for members of parliament, the system elects multiple winners.

Indian Electoral System:
The Constitution of India has vested in the Election Commission of India the Superintendence, direction and control of the entire process for conduct of elections to Parliament and Legislature of every State and to the offices of President and Vice-President of India. The Indian Electoral system has been broadly divided into two, they are Direct election based on territorial constituencies and Proportional representation by means of a single transferable vote. The first system is followed for the election of the members of Lok Sabha, State Assemblies and Union Territories'assemblies. The second, election held on the basis of proportional representation by means of a single transferable vote for the President and the Vice-President of India, members of Rajya Sabha and members of Legislative councils.

The main features of Indian electoral system:

1. Elections are held on the basis of Universal adult franchise. Who is a citizen of India and not less than 18 years of age can register as a voter in electoral roll of India. There is no discrimination on the ground of religion, race, caste, sex or any of them.

2. There is a provision for reservation of seats for Scheduled Castes (84 Seats) and Scheduled Tribes(47 Seats) in Lok Sabha and Assemblies of State and Union Territories, but there is no such provision of reservations in Rajya Sabha at the Union level and Legislative councils at the State level.

3. For the general seats representation is accorded on territorial basis through common electoral roll. Constituencies are delimited with the help of a delimitation commissions (1952, 1963, 1973 and 2002) which is appointed after the census that takes place after every ten years .The result of the revision of constituencies is that that the areas/boundaries change from election to election, but the number of constituencies will not be changed up to the year 2026.

4. Voting takes place through secret ballot for the Lok Sabha and State assemblies. It is most important and prerequisite to the public to express their will freely and fairly. For the Rajya Sabha and Council of States through the open ballot system is introduced to stop the corruption in those elections.

5. Political parties are an indispensable part of the electoral process. In India multi party system is functioning.

Redressal

The redressal for any doubts and disputes arising out of the elections to the office of the President of India and the Vice-President of India lie with the Supreme Court.

For doubts and disputes arising out of elections to the offices of Parliament and State Legislatures, the High Court serves as the initial jurisdiction. There is a provision to appeal to the Supreme Court if needed.

For matters relating to the elections to municipalities and other local bodies, the lower courts are entrusted with resolving disputes in accordance with the laws enacted by the concerned State Government.

Acts and Rules relating to the Election Laws

- **Presidential and Vice-Presidential Elections Act 1952**

This act was enacted by the Indian Parliament for the election to the offices of President and Vice-President of India.

- **Presidential and Vice-Presidential Elections Rules 1974**

This is a supplementary set of rules to the Presidential and Vice-Presidential Elections Act 1952.

- **Representation of the People Act 1950**

This Act governs the conduct of elections to State Legislatures and to Parliament. This act is concerned with the preparation of electoral rolls and their revisions.

- **The Registration of Electors Rules 1960**

Under Section 28 of the Act, these rules were made by the Central Government along with the Election Commission, and supplements the provisions of this act with detailed rules. All rules relating to the preparation of electoral rolls, their periodic updating and revision fall under this provision. It provides for the registration of eligible electors and the issue of voter ID cards or electoral identity cards with the voter's photograph. It also includes rules on the inclusion of eligible voters, the exclusion of ineligible voters and any corrections required. With these rules, the Election Commission is empowered to prepare the photo electoral rolls which will contain the name, photograph and other particulars of the electors.

- **Representation of the People Act 1951**

This Act governs the actual conduct of elections to State Legislatures and to Parliament. According to this Act, all post election matters that comprise of doubts and disputes that arise out of the elections or are in connection with the elections, will be dealt with in accordance to the provisions of this Act. All disputes can be raised in the High Court of the respective State. These post election matters can be raised after the election is over and not during the process of it.

- **Conduct of Elections Rules 1961**

These rules were framed under Section 169 of the Act by the Central Government along with the Election Commission. It deals with detailed rules for every stage of the conduct of elections. It encompassses the issue of the writ notification for conducting elections, filing of nominations, and the scrutiny of the nominations. It also deals with withdrawal of candidates. Taking the polls and counting votes are also governed by these rules. Finally, the constitution of the Houses based on the results are also categorised under these rules.

Model Code of Conduct

Under Article 324 of the Constitution of India, the Election Commission has the right to exercise its power in the enforcement of the Model Code of Conduct. This Code is a unique document which helps guide political candidates and parties. The Model Code of Conduct was created by the political parties to ensure fair elections for all parties involved. It governs matters related to conduct and the maintenance of a level playing field throughout the elections. It also provides for rules against the misuse of official machinery and power by the ruling party to ensure that they do not unfairly further the electoral prospects of their own candidates.

The Acts and Rules listed above empower the Election Commission to issue directives to deal with different aspects involved with the preparation of electoral rolls, its revision and the actual conduct of elections. All grievance related to the elections will have to be resolved under the Representation of the People Acts 1950 and 1951, and the Registration of Electors Rules 1960 and Conduct of Elections Rules 1961. These Acts and Rules form a complete set of rules and a code for all matters relating to the elections to the State Legislatures and Houses of Parliament.

ElectronicVotingMachines(EVMs)

EVMs have been used successfully in limited areas in sensitive constituencies and in bye-elections. Any doubts about this technology were amply removed during the deliberations of the Goswami Committee. Not only were the EVMs satisfactorily demonstrated to all politician members, several electronic experts of the Government of India also testified that the machines could be used at all our elections without any misgivings. The advantages of EVMs in preventing large-scale rigging are quite apparent as the machine locks up and will permit only one hit every so many seconds. Wherever these EVMs have been used in urban and in rural areas, there have been no complaints of large scale rigging. This also makes counting easy and non-contestable and theoretically the results could be available within a very short time if the system wanted to make prompt announcement of the winning candidates.

Postal voting

Postal voting in India is done only through the "Electronically Transmitted Postal Ballot Papers (ETPB)" system of Election Commission of India, where ballot papers are distributed to the registered eligible voters and they return the votes by post. When the counting of votes commences, these postal votes are counted before those from the Electronic Voting Machines. Only certain categories of people are eligible to register as postal voters. People working in the Union armed forces and state police as well as their spouses, and employees working for the Government of India who are officially posted abroad can register for the postal vote, these are also called the "Service voters". Additionally, people in preventive detention, disabled and those above the age of 80 years old can use postal vote. Prisoners can not vote at all.

Conclusion

Democracy can have its true meaning only when the large mass of people turnout to vote because as the 16th President of United States of America has stated that , " Government of the people, by the people and for the people" (this was said by him in his Gettysburg Address) . This clearly means that people are the true essence of democracy. Therefore, to make India democracy in true sense the voting turnout needs to be increased. In my view following steps can be taken to increase the voter turnout-

• The voters belonging to the urban working middle class can be given the incentive that who ever votes can get an extra day of paid leave this could further be added in the corporate bodies Corporate Social Responsibility.

• The voters need to be educated that every vote matters. The students can be educated how a single vote can make difference.

• For the people living in rural areas the literacy needs to be increased and government should organise drives to educate the people.

• The National Commission of Women can take steps to ensure the safety of women and carry out gender sensitization drives to generate awareness about voting among women.

• The government should deploy more security and ensure safety of the boots in every way possible. In my view, the process of election can also be reformed and both the elections to the Lok Sabha and the State Legislatures could be made to take place at the same time. This will decrease the expenditure needed in conducting the election and it can cause to form a stable government in every state and ensure that there is no fall of government in the next five years, as is in the case of most Coalition Governments.

VIII

Plea bargaining in Criminal Justice system: National and International legal perspective. [Author- Dr. Anju Choudhary.] [Co-Author- Ms. Mehak.]

William Edwart Gladstone, former Prime Minister of the United Kingdom, quoted *"Justice delayed is justice denied"*[1], this phrase very clearly means that if justice is not accomplished within a reasonable time period then even if it is accomplished later on then the justice is not said to be real. Indian judiciary is the most important pillars of democracy. Being an independent organ of the government, people look up to judiciary as the least corrupted and the one that stands for the people of India. Thus, the citizens approach the courts in order to get justice, whenever their rights are violated. But due to certain reasons such as explosion of litigation, accumulation of first appeal, inadequacy of staff i.e. vacancy crisis in Indian Judiciary, granting of unnecessary adjournments, indiscriminate closure of Courts and inordinate delay in the supply of certified copies of judgments and orders etc causes unnecessary delays in providing justice to the society. *"Justice Hurried is Justice Buried[2]"*is just similar to the phrase 'Justice Delayed is Justice Denied', true i.e. if a justice is given in a rush without following proper procedure, it is too violation of the principal of natural justice. Consequently, adequate rational and appropriate hearing, depending on the circumstances of the case is required according to the principal of natural justice. After taking into consideration the load of long-lasting cases on the Judiciary plea bargaining was introduced in Criminal Justice System of India.

The Concept of Plea Bargaining was first time adopted in America and eventually the Indian Criminal Justice System also introduced Plea Bargaining to the Criminal Procedure Code of India by adding up a new chapter XXIA (Section 265A - 265L) under the Criminal Procedure (Amendment) Act, 2005. Plea Bargaining is a replacement to long-lasting and complicated process of trial in courts that guarantees reduction in overcrowding of courts and speedy disposal of cases. Recently, citizens of some countries were charged for infringing the guidelines of government subsequent to the Covid-19 widespread and visa terms, all such persons were released from such charges according to plea bargaining procedure[3].

1.2 HISTORICAL DEVELOPMENT OF PLEA BARGANING

The adoption of the concept of plea bargaining was from the American practice followed in leading case of *"**Brady vs. United States**"*[4], it was carried out that granting profit to the accused also imparts profit to the state. This judgment acknowledged some of the minimum requirements for plea bargaining; firstly, the trial should be held in courts, secondly, the court should be fully satisfied that the defendant wants to plead guilty, the plea must be made intelligently, the court must ensure that there must be a factual basis for entering in to guilty plea and any order rejecting plea bargaining must be kept confidential. Further, in **"Sanobello vs. New York"[5]** the Supreme Court of United States accepted finally that plea bargaining is a crucial part of administration of justice when appropriately operated and the practice of plea bargaining must be encouraged.

In India initially, the judiciary was reluctant in introducing the concept of plea bargaining in India. The **"Kachhia Patel Shantilal Koderlal vs. State of Gujarat and Anr"[6]**Apex Court criticized plea bargaining being against the law as it would likely to promote corruption in the process of delivering justice. Further, the Apex Court in **"Kasambhai vs. State of Gujarat"[7]**, expressed that such practice of plea bargaining is likely to be maltreated.

Recommendation in order to introduce 'Plea Bargaining' was made in 142nd, 154th and 177th Report of the Law Commission of India. In its 154th Report of the Law Commission recommended of adding up a new Chapter XXIA to the Criminal Procedure Code of India, while referring the 142nd Report in which justification behind plea bargaining, its successful functioning in the USA and the method in which it should be given a statutory shape. The Report while recommending said that this particular concept should be made pertinent as a preliminary step for offences that are punishable with imprisonment for less than seven years and fine along with the offences enclosed under section 320 of this Criminal Procedure Code. Further, it was also recommended that this concept is not accessible to conventional criminals, persons charged with grave socio-economic offences and any offences committed against women and children. Furthermore, Malimath Committee also in its Report recommended reformation in Criminal justice system, 2000 similar to the procedure of United States on plea bargaining for disposing off the gathered cases and accelerating justice delivery system.

Eventually, the Parliament initiated the draft of Criminal Law (Amendment) Bill, 2003 and it was enforceable since July 5, 2006. The Act amended the provisions of Indian Evidence Act, 1892, Indian Penal Code 1860 and the Code of Criminal Procedure, 1973 for the purpose of improving the prevailing Indian Criminal Justice System. The important issues that were focused in Criminal Law (Amendment) Bill, 2003 were: whilst the witnesses changes hostile, combining the violation under Section 498A of IPC and confirmation in matters concerning to fake currency notes and scientific experts and practicing of Plea-bargaining. Based on these recommendations, a new Chapter XXIA, Section 265A to 265L was introduced and brought the concept of plea bargaining in India[8]

1.3 CONCEPT OF PLEA BARGANING

Plea Bargaining refers pre-trail negotiation in which a person accused of a crime by pleading himself guilty to a less serious offence negotiates for a lower punishment than what is given under the law. It is also known as pre-trail settlement, plea negotiation, resolution discussion; mutually satisfactory disposition etc. Very briefly, Plea Bargaining therefore means "Pleading Guilty and Bargaining for Lesser Sentence". As a rule, "plea bargaining" may be described as negotiations prior to the trail among the accused and the victim. It is generally carried out by the pleader, wherein the accused accepts to plead guilty in turn for specific concessions from the prosecutor.

Kinds of plea bargaining: Plea bargaining is of three kinds mainly and each of these involves reduction of sentence impliedly but it differs in the methods of achieving these reductions. Following are the kinds of plea bargaining:

1. Charge bargaining: In such a bargain a defendant pleads guilty to reduce specific charges that he will face during the trail.
2. Sentence bargaining: In this kind of bargain it implies assurance of lesser or some substitute sentence to the accused in return of pleading guilty.

3. Fact bargaining: In this kind of bargain, negotiations are made for the admission of some facts with an agreement not to introduce other facts reciprocally.

1.4 NATIONAL AND INTERNATIONAL LEGAL PERSPECIVE ON PLEA BARGAIING

At International Level

Plea Bargaining in United States of America

In United States of America acknowledgement to the concept of Plea Bargaining was given by the judiciary in the matter of **"Santebello vs. New York[9]"** and "*Brady vs. United States[10]*". The Supreme Court of USA has established that in order to make plea bargaining legally valid, both prosecutor and defendant must consider all the terms and conditions of the agreement made during the negotiation. Consequently, negotiations while exercising plea bargains must be permitted by the judge so as to consider it legally binding. Furthermore, such decision should support the verity that if in case agreement of the plea bargains are breached remedies will be available for that even though it has not been prescribed by the Court.

Plea Bargaining in United Kingdom

Pointing out the pressure of case load, thus making the trail procedure more lengthy, plea bargaining was introduced in the administration of criminal justice system of United Nation. Formerly, the practice of plea bargaining invariably took place in England behind closed doors. There used to be unofficial bargains by way of discount in sentence and the charge getting decreased. Plea agreements negotiated by the Serious Fraud Office of United Kingdom can be considered as the initial or primary form of plea bargaining in United Kingdom. Thomas LJ in **"Innospec"[11]**, observed that the course of action in which agreements are made while pleading guilty and consequently the imposition of fine is thoroughly incompetent. Therefore, there is a strong need to exhibit a more detailed examination regarding the character of exercising of plea bargain agreements. Exercise of plea bargaining is necessarily against or beyond the scope of serious cases of fraud and ergo plea agreements are not introduced in such kind of cases.

In "***R v Turner***"[12] the UK courts while remarking the practice of plea bargaining came up with the rules to gear up the controversy of plea agreements, accordingly, it was observed that the Counsel must be entirely free to do his duty such as giving the best possible advice to the accused and such advice may also include advice of pleading of guilt.

Further, a statutory scheme was imported namely Serious Organised Crime and Police Act 2005 wherein, provisions were laid down regarding an established privilege of making n agreements between the investigating team and the accused.

Pre-charge bargaining has come out as an evolving concept in fraud cases. This is because in fraud cases of plea bargaining it is necessary for the defendant to initiate or start a plea before the proceedings of the trail has been started in fraud office. The so-called logic behind this is that fraud cases are very tricky to discover and somewhat costly to examine and inspect. Therefore, the practice of plea bargaining in such situations gives could profit to both the victims and jurors.

Plea Bargaining in Australia

The concept of the Plea bargaining is an accepted practice in the criminal justice system of Australia. An open approach of plea bargaining favours the accused and the community as well. The plea bargaining system of Australia may be divided into two types i.e. Charge bargaining and sentence indication bargaining. Sentence implication bargaining is exceptionally exercised in Australia as compared to charge bargaining. In addition to these two, some authors also express the practice of implicit plea bargaining in the Australian criminal justice. In the implicit plea bargaining or tacit type of plea bargaining unexpressed and latent influence is made on the offender.

Prosecution is one of the most important parties while making the decision in the pre-trial hearing. The prosecutor is only one who has been assigned to make a decision regarding the charge against the offender. Under the Australian system of plea bargaining the court does not have any opportunity to interfere in the pre-trial decision making procedure. According to the foundation f the criminal procedure of Australia, the Judge is the only authority who can levy sentence on the offender after considering and investigating the necessary facts of the case[13]. While declaring the final decision, the sentencing judge is not bound to give the decision as per the agreement of the negotiation between the parties; rather the judge is having the discretion to give the decision other than the agreement in the interest of the society.

Further, in order to maintain openness and congnizability of the plea bargaining records of the negotiations must be made in the written form.

At National Level: Plea Bargaining in India

Plea Bargaining was introduced in the India's Criminal Procedure Code by adding a new chapter that is Chapter XXIA including Sections 265A to 265L. Accordingly, under this chapter exercise of plea bargaining is allowed in the matters where defendant above 18 years and the one against whom trial is pending, he can submit an application for plea bargaining[14]. Plea bargaining cannot be invoked in every case. It is subject to the following:-

1. Available in cases the maximum punishment for such offence is imprisonment below 7 years.
2. Defendant must not commit a crime against any women or any child under the age of 14 years.
3. The defendant pleading guilty must be 18 years above.
4. The defendant pleading guilty must not be convicted in prior for that same crime.
5. The defendant pleading guilty must not have committed a crime that influences negatively the socio-economic environment of India.
6. Further, defendant pleading guilty is not eligible for plea bargaining if any crime committed by him sinking under

Protection of Women from Domestic Violence Act, Dowry prohibition Act, Protection of Civil Rights Act, Armed Forces Act Essential Commodities Act, etc.

The accused along with the application for plea bargaining has to submit an affidavit declaring that he understands the nature of the proceedings under plea bargaining. On receiving such an application the judge issues notice to the public prosecutor[15]. The proceedings under plea bargaining are tried in camera. After the complete satisfaction of the court, the defendant can voluntarily file an application asking for an opportunity to work out with the victim and mutually decide the matter[16]. This means the accused must be willing to provide the victim compensation and any such expenses which the victim may wish. When a meeting of all the parties has been accomplished, a report may be submitted before the court duly signed by the Presiding Officers, defendant and the victim. If on the other hand nothing has been decided mutually then the court must record such observation and proceed according to the provisions of Cr PC[17]. If in case a mutually satisfactory agreement has been accomplished, then the court may dispose off matter. Prior to dispose the matter off the court should also check that compensation has been awarded to the victim. Further the court must give opportunity to the defendant for deciding the amount of sentence.

1. The defendant may be released on probation of good conduct or after admonition by the court.
2. The court may award minimum punishment such as half of the punishment according to law.
3. The court can also award any such punishment to the defendant, if the offence is not covered under Section 265 (b) & (c).
4. In computing the sentence of the accused, the courts are permitted to set off the period of detention undergone by the accused.

Ultimately, after the satisfaction of the court, a Judgment will be pronounced by the court after both the parties have mutually agreed on the negotiation[18]. Further, there shall be no appeal against such judgment other than a Special Leave Petition[19] or a writ petition[20] can be filed. Furthermore, concept of plea bargaining as provided in the Indian Criminal Justice System, does not include any child or juvenile or as demarcated in Section 2 clause (k) of Juvenile Justice Act, 2000[21].

A Comparative Analysis of Plea Bargaining at International and National Level:

Although plea bargaining is essentially similar in India as well America, but at the same time there are some significant differences as well such as; firstly, in the USA, plea bargaining can be opted by the defendant for any offence he or she has been charged with. Whereas, in India plea bargaining a defendant can opt for plea bargaining only when the crime committed by him has maximum punishment for not more than seven years. Secondly, in USA, negotiations among prosecutor and parties are done out of the court. Whereas, in India, to initiate negotiations the defendant has to file an application so as to minimize the chance of duress. Thirdly, in India application for plea bargaining will be admissible only when judge is fully satisfied and believes that such punishment consented for in plea bargaining is not reached out by the of unfairness or the court may set aside the application otherwise. Whereas, in USA no such rule is present.

Further, in some common law countries such as UK and Australia, the concept of plea bargaining is permissible only if the prosecutors and the defence mutually decides that the offender would be pleading guilty for few charges and in return the prosecutor will give up the rest. Furthermore, some Civil law jurisdictions like China, Georgia, Italy, France, Germany, Denmark, and Japan, finds it challenging while applying the practice of plea bargaining in their criminal justice system as because in civil law no conception of plea is discussed. Nevertheless, of all the difficulties civil law countries have began to apply this concept within their systems by modifying their legal framework.

1.5 JUDICIAL APPROACH TOWARDS PLEA BARGAINING

The Indian judiciary was initially unwilling to adopt the concept of plea bargaining. In a number of cases the Supreme Court has criticized this practice being invalid in spite of the recommendations of the Law Commission and the Malimath Committee.

The Apex Court in ***"Kasambhai vs State of Gujarat"*[22]**& **"*Kachhia Patel Shantilal Koderlal vs State of Gujarat and Anr*[23]"** observed that the exercise of Plea Bargaining is in contrast to the public policy and interest of the community. Further, this Court declared that exercising plea bargaining is somehow unconstitutional as it tend to promote the corruption and might pollute the source of justice. Supreme Court has ceaselessly opined that the concept and exercise of plea bargaining is unconstitutional and likely to promote corruption between the negotiating parties. Justice Bhagwati in **"*Thippaswamy v. State of Karnataka* [24]**, held that plea bargaining is unmistakably violative of Article 21, of the Constitution as it persuades the accused to plead guilty with guarantee that he would be discharged or relived with a lighter or reduced punishment.

The Apex Court has always criticized the initiation of plea bargaining in criminal justice system. In the case of **"*State of Uttar Pradesh v. Chandrika*"[25]**, it was observed by the Supreme Court that the very foundation or base of plea bargaining cannot eliminate the criminal cases as the courts have to still make a decision according to the circumstances of the case. Further, it was also held that the exercise of plea bargaining interferes with the welfare and interest of the public as it decides the case against the given legislative provisions.

Further, the Apex Court in **"*State Of Gujarat vs Natwar Harchandji Thakor*"[26]**, recognized the significance of plea bargaining, and observed that "plea of guilty" must be elucidated as a part of statutory process at the time of criminal trial. Therefore, while considering the dynamic character of the society and law, it was observed by the court that the reason to add this concept in the criminal justice system is to supply an easy, cheap and expeditious justice for resolving the disputes.

Furthermore, in the case of ***"State of Gujarat v Natwar Harchanji Thakor"***[27] the Gujarat High Court welcomed the practice of plea bargaining procedure and declared that the actual purpose of initiating the law of plea bargaining was to furnish prompt and speedy justice of the disputes. As plea bargaining adds a new scope is in the domain of judicial reforms."

1.6 CONCLUSION AND SUGGESSTIONS

Coming to the conclusion, without doubt plea bargaining can be undoubtedly, is a powerful tool to reduce the pending cases and thus aiding in quick administration of justice. Plea bargaining may elude an offender both the conviction and stigma connected along with. Further, the society also benefits from practice of this concept as the cases are disposed of quickly and more efficiently. Notable lags in the administration of justice by the judiciary can be addressed conveniently. Expenditure of trials and structure of judiciary are decreased.

Plea barraging is a controversial concept. Some groups have appreciated it while others some have rejected it. Although it is correct to say that plea bargaining helps in speeding up caseload disposition but at the same time it also correct to say that it does so in an unconstitutional and illegal approach. But conceivably we do not have any other option than to embrace this method. Since, the criminal courts are overcrowded it becomes very tough to permit every single matter to go for trial.

The Indian judiciary was initially not in favour of implementing the concept of plea bargaining being unconstitutional against the principle of natural justice. Despite that, the parliament by making an amendment under the Criminal law (amendment) act, 2005 incorporated a new chapter XXIA in the Cr.P.C. 1973. Even though this concept is a part of the Indian criminal justice system for roughly 15-16 years, this has not become an accepted method of dispute resolution. One of the reason behind such non acceptance is lack of knowledge and awareness among the citizens or lack of interest of courts. The concept of plea bargaining in United States is therefore seen as a best example for other countries since the application of plea bargaining by the American Criminal justice system has succeeded in reducing the pendency and over burden of criminal cases in criminal courts of United States. Even after such accomplishment some jurists still criticizes this concept condemned for being illegal and ineffective method of handling criminal cases. The primary disagreement is that in the contemporary world where approximately all the legal frameworks follows the reformative theory of punishment there exercise plea bargaining is considered against such system. Nonetheless, there is a necessity for understanding this concept of plea bargaining so that huge amount of pendency of the cases can be reduced. As more appropriately it can be also be understood by saying that "Some justice is better than No Justice"

Therefore, the concept of Plea Bargaining can be considered as technique of convenience and reciprocal profits rather than a question of constitutionality. There is an inevitable requirement to bring an essential alteration in the administration of criminal justice scheme. This practice of plea bargaining can be appreciated only when there is probability of reasonably priced resolution of cases. So, if the main aim criminal justice system is to recover and fit the criminals back in the society by making them go though specific punishment then the concept of plea bargaining does comes in use. Thus, placing the concept of plea bargaining underneath judicial analysis may unlock the prospect of fair transactions in such bargains. Conversely in order to get the benefit of this concept and further to protect the benefits of such reforms concept of plea bargaining can be effectively used. Advocates defending the matter must advice and persuade his clients to opt negotiations under the process of plea bargaining rather than to thinking of their professional gain. Apparently that the ability of constructing the police and judges must be considered as a main concern and precondition while exercising plea bargaining. From the practice plea bargaining in United States it can be believed and understood that the practice of plea bargaining continues to be a disputed doubtful concept. At the same time, looking on to the excess numbers of criminal cases in the courts are piling up the fundamentals and principles of plea bargaining may be acknowledged as one of the vital methods of speeding up caseload on the courts. As a delay in justice my lead to various repercussions which may be experienced by both the victim and the accused and would eventually be a failure of justice. Therefore, in order to apply this method of trail in the administration of criminal justice system, more awareness among the people regarding the benefits of this concept and proper implementation of the laws by the organs of the government must be encouraged.

[1]https://www.legalserviceindia.com/legal/article-3313-justice-delayed-is-justice-denied.html, (Visited on August 17, 2021)

[2] ibid

[3]   https://www.drishtiias.com/daily-updates/daily-news-analysis/plea-bargaining, (Visited on August 17, 2021)

[4] 397 U.S. 742 (1970)

[5] 404 U.S. 257 (1971)

[6] 1980CriLJ553

[7] (1980 AIR 854)

[8] Benny Paul, *Simplified Approach of Criminal Procedure Code* 285 (Shree Ram Law House, Chandigarh edn., 2018).

[9] ibid

[10] ibid

[11] [2017] UKSC 47

[12] [1970] 2 QB 321

[13]   https://www.worldwidejournals.com/paripex/article/a-comparative-study-on-plea-bargaining-in-india-and-other-countries/MTAxNTQ=/?is=1, (Visited on September 3, 2021)

[14] Section 265A of The Code of Criminal Procedure, 1973(Act 2 of 1974)

[15] 265B of The Code of Criminal Procedure, 1973(Act 2 of 1974)

[16] 265D of The Code of Criminal Procedure, 1973(Act 2 of 1974)

[17] 265E of The Code of Criminal Procedure, 1973(Act 2 of 1974)

[18] 265 F of The Code of Criminal Procedure, 1973(Act 2 of 1974)

[19] Article 136 of The Indian Constitution, 1950

[20] Article 226 or 227 of The Indian Constitution, 1950

[21] Section 265-L of The Code of Criminal Procedure, 1973(Act 2 of 1974)

[22] ibid

[23] ibid

[24] 3 1976 Cr.L.J 1527

[25] 2000 Cr.L.J. 384(386); AIR 2000 SC 164

[26] (2005) 1 GLR 709

[27] 9 (2005) Cr.L.J. 2957

IX

Crime Scene investigation & Technicians. [Author: Garima Oberoi] [Co Author: Ankush Garg]

Criminal law has been constantly evolving and forensic science had been a greater part of solving crimes and bringing criminals to justice. Forensic science means the convergence of science and technology into solving crimes thereby aiding the criminal justice system. Forensic scientists or criminalistics have aided the justice system immensely providing precise and objective information helping in connecting crime, recreating crime scenes, and also in identifying criminals.

The commencement of forensic science in the crime scene can be dated back to 3rd Century China when burning pattern was studied to solve a crime which was found in the manuscript called " *A Collection of Criminal Cases*" by YU YU JI. Very noteworthy historical criminalistics includes *Francois Emanuel Fodore*who specialized in detecting arsenic toxins in corpses; *Mathieu Orfila* who was called the father of forensic technology also specialized in the detection of poisons in early 1814. The most prominent and important pioneer is from the 20th century *Edmond Locard*, who introduced the very famous "LOCARD'S EXCHANGE PRINCIPLE"[1].

PROCESSING A CRIME SCENE:

A crime scene is the place of occurrence of a criminal event, where the application of forensics and the work of criminalists begins. Processing the crime scene is recreating the events that have occurred in that particular place and properly collecting the physical evidence. Physical evidence is the objects found in and around the crime scene that helps forensic technicians to connect a person to the crime[2]. Processing a crime scene and properly collecting the physical evidence is very pivotal for a technician to deduce a crime.

The investigating officer is the first to arrive at a crime scene. He has the primary duty of securing the crime scene and keeping the crime scene intact. Keeping the crime scene undisturbed is very pivotal for an investigating officer. An undisturbed crime scene is easier to work with for forensic technicians to recreate the events that occurred and to evaluate the physical evidence. The investigating officer should record the crime scene in its original state by taking photographs, sketches, and notes. The investigating officer also records the state of the victim before the medical officer arrives at the crime scene[3].

The evidence is collected using variable collection methods which are done by forensic technicians. Each piece of evidence is numbered and packaged and sent to forensic crime labs for evaluation. A different medium of packaging intact evidence is practiced by the technicians like in evidence bags, druggist fold collection, and zip locks for solid evidence. All this physical evidence is sent to forensic laboratories and after evaluation done by technicians, the evidence along with the laboratory findings are submitted to the court under the chain of custody for interpretation by the court[4].

RECONSTRUCTION OF CRIME SCENE AND THE ROLE OF FORENSIC TECHNICIANS:

Reconstructing a crime scene is an important modus operandi to solve a crime. Reconstruction, to state is to reorder or reestablish the events in a previous state to understand the event that had occurred in the area where any sort of crime had occurred. Reconstruction of any criminal event can be done with the help of forensic analysts by analyzing various physical evidence. The sequence of events is analyzed by various forensic technicians arriving at the crime or present in a laboratory and they ascertain these findings to connect a person to the crime. Linkage or Transfer patterns found in a crime scene are sequenced accordingly by the various forensic technicians eg. For, finding bloodstain patterns in a crime scene could the analysts able to tell the weapon used to cause the blood spread pattern, finding hair strands could help analyze DNA evidence connecting to the criminal, semen analysis is also done by the technicians to prove sexual assault crimes[5]. An invariable number of forensic technicians are called for to help solve the crime and to reconstruct the crime scene which is highly used in the court to bring justice to the victims of violent crimes.

MAJOR FORENSIC TECHNICIANS IN AID
FINGERPRINT ANALYSIS EXPERT

Fingerprint analysis is very important and primary detection at a crime scene. An early pioneer in utilizing this technique dates back to *HENRY FAULDS*, he found the potential application of fingerprints by studying the skin ridge patterns. In 1892, *GALTON* published a book called FINGERPRINTS in which he described the anatomy of fingerprints[6]. The Federal Bureau of Investigation, USA, was the first investigative unit to adopt a fingerprint identification system in the year 1924. FBI has the largest collection of fingerprints in its Integrated Automatic & Fingerprint Identification System [IAFIS][7].

The very first admissibility of Fingerprint as evidence connecting a crime can be dated back to 1999 in the case ***United***

States v Byron C Mitchell,in this particular case, happened in the Eastern District of Pennsylvania, the honorable Judge upheld the admissibility of fingerprint as evidence. The judge also highlighted two important aspects to the admissibility of fingerprints as evidence i.e a. Human finger ridges are unique and permanent 2. The arrangement of these skin ridges is unique and permanent[8].

The experts in analyzing the diversification of fingerprints are called latent print examiners or forensic fingerprint experts. Their primary obligation involves gathering the fingerprint from the crime scene and making a comparative analysis of the fingerprint to associate a person with the crime scene.

The fundamental principle behind fingerprint analysis involves the identification of furrows and ridges in the fingers, toes, and palms in the retrieved fingerprint from the crime scene. The fingerprint patterns are majorly classified into three patterns which are unique to every individual. Those unique patterns are *Loops, Whorls & Arches*, these patterns remain as such and do not show any change in the lifetime of a person under any circumstances[9].

Forensic fingerprint experts have two major duties in solving a crime. The first duty is the collection of the fingerprint from the crime scene. The collection of fingerprints involves a more methodical process to retrieve the fingerprint carefully. Forensic experts have classified three types of surfaces where fingerprints are retrieved. Fingerprint form soft surfaces, and fingerprint form hard surfaces which are further classified into latent and patent prints. Latent prints are hard to extract as they are not readily visible and require chemical agents, powders, and potent light sources to identify and retrieve those latent prints[10].

Fingerprint experts use high-resolution digital cameras to take photographs of fingerprints. Light sources are used at a specific wavelength to find latent prints in door knobs, handles, etc. Chemical developers are also used by the technicians like ninhydrin which imparts purple color on the latent prints. Amido Black, a non-specific protein stain is used to retrieving prints from very difficult surfaces[11].

Once the fingerprints are retrieved from these surfaces at a crime scene, the experts analyze them by comparing known fingerprints from huge databases and also from suspects to identify the person to whom these prints belong. These evaluations are then presented to the court for interpretation.

FORENSIC BALLISTIC EXPERTS

Arms and their fragments are likely to be found at a crime scene if weapons are used to commit a crime. These weapons can also be studied and can be used by experts to identify their origin and the type of weapon used to commit a crime. Ballistic Forensic Experts are those professionals who study the weapons and their fragments from a crime scene. The ballistic analysis includes the study of motion, dynamics, angular momentum, and the effect of a projectile unit on a weapon[12].

Ballistics experts help invariably in the identification of weapons. Ballistic experts study the residues from the weapon and they aid in the identification of different types of guns. They help in the linkage of the crime scene to the weapon used, identify the position of the perpetrator, and also in studying different striations found on the bullets.

Ballistics experts are imparted with the duty to study, analyze and examine bullets, their fragments, cartridges, etc. Firearms exert different patterns which are unique for each weapon and it helps the ballistic expert to identify the shooter[13].

There are four types of ballistic studies involving different parts of the ballistic analysis of firearms. It includes Internal, External, Terminal, and Transitional Ballistics in each the expert studies different types of motions in a firearm and the effect of its projectile[14]. Comparison Microscopy is highly used by experts to study the distinctions and striations patterns in the bullets.

The very first case which utilized forensic ballistics experts can be dated back to 1835 wherein *Henry Herbert Goddard*, the father of ballistics, used his expertise to identify a bullet and be able to distinguish the peculiarity of the bullet by detecting a small deformation in its manufacturing and be able to connect the bullet with the culprit[15].

FORENSIC TOXICOLOGISTS

Forensic Toxicology is another pivotal branch of forensic science that aid in the criminal justice system. Forensic Toxicologists recognize various types of drugs and poisons from body fluids, tissues, and organs.

Individuals are nowadays highly exposed to drugs and toxins via voluntary ingestion, by accident, suicide, and also used as means for committing murder. Many individuals are also involved in substance abuse to impart hallucinations. Even substance abuse may cause death by overdose and toxicologists to help in identifying the type of drug abuse.

Poisons are also a huge cause of death in the country. They are used as means of murder and also ingested by individuals to commit suicide. There is a wide range of poisonous substances that are being consumed and exposed by the public. Some of the common poisons are classified based on their chemical composition, physiology, and their method of extraction. There exist seven classifications of common poisons which covers an enormous multiplicity of poisons and substances. Those includes[16]:

1. ANIONS: They can be found commonly in weedicides, bleaching agents, and insecticides. Eg. CYANIDE POISONING
2. CORROSIVE POISONS: These type of poisons includes a wide range of Acids and Alkalis that can destroy tissues on contact. Eg. Hydrochloric Acid [HCl], Sulphuric Acid [H_2SO_3], and Pottasium Hydroxide [KOH].
3. GASEOUS & VOLATILE POISONS: The main characteristic of this type of poison is that it turns into vapor at room temperature. The major cause of death in case of accidental fires like gas explosions, water heater explosions, etc. The gaseous substance released is toxic and proves fatal to individuals who are exposed. Eg. Carbon Monoxide poisoning causes death by asphyxiation

4. METAL & METALLOID POISONS: The individuals are exposed to these categories of poisons mostly from industries. Toxicologists determine the presence of these poisons using the Reinsch test by dipping a copper strip in the victim's body fluids which will impart a silvery or dark coat over the inserted copper strip. Eg. Arsenic, Lithium, Antimony, Lead, etc

5. PESTICIDES: A very common exposure to poisons by individuals is pesticides. Pesticides are highly used as means of suicide in many rural areas. Eg. the Most common pesticide poisons are from the category of Organophosphate compounds.

6. TOXINS: These are the substances that are produced by living organisms like plants, animals, and microbes. Major exposure to the toxin is from food consumption which is contaminated with the toxins. Eg. Aconitine, Atropine, Strychnine, etc.

7. DRUGS OF ABUSE: Drugs that are commonly and illicitly abused by individuals to cause hallucinations as means of pleasure. These drugs are produced illegally and are consumed by most of the population. They affect the central nervous system and cause hallucinations in an individual. Death of people by drug overdose can be seen invariably. Eg. Alcohol, heroin, cocaine, Amphetamines, etc

The Role of Toxicologists is to single out these drugs by using various analytical methods. The common method of analysis used by toxicologists are A. ascertainment of physical properties of drugs B. Presumptive test by using reagents for the detection of colors which are unique to every compounds C. Thin Layer Chromatographic technique to separate drugs from bulk sample D. Immunoassay are performed to extract highly specific results E. GC-MS [Gas Chromatography coupled with Mass Spectrometer] analysis provides precise detection of drugs from trace amounts[17]. Toxicologists collect blood, urine, and hair samples from the victim or suspect and identify the amount of drug consumed, type of substance abused, and substance used to commit homicide.

FORENSIC MEDICINE & FORENSIC ODONTOLOGY:

Forensic Medicine is an exceedingly valuable stream of Forensic Science that resorts to Medical knowledge in aiding the Criminal Justice System. Forensic Medical Examiners utilize their skills in identifying crimes against humans. These Forensic Medical Examiners also act as expert witnesses in the court.

The importance of forensic medicine and admissibility as expert evidence can be dated back to the 6th Century AD in the Roman Empire wherein *Justinian Code* was enacted which tends to regulate medical practice and their expertise being utilized in legal procedures. Later in the year 1302, the first medicolegal autopsy was performed in Bologna, Italy. In the year 1553, *Emperor Charles V* of Germany enacted *Caroline Code* in which emphasis was laid on medical expert testimony in homicides[18].

Forensic Medical examiners have the primary duty to identify the victim and to deduce the cause and time of death. They perform an autopsy on the victims to collect vital clues about the cause of death and to identify the crime.

A clinical Autopsy is performed by the Medical examiners to determine the following aspects of the death of an individual [19]:

- To identify the body
- To estimate the exact time of death
- To identify the different types of injuries present in the body
- To identify the nature and the total number of injuries
- To identify the significance of injuries, whether it was the means to cause the death of the individual
- To identify the presence of any previous or predetermined disease in the individual
- To identify the presence of any toxic substance
- To identify the effect of any medical treatment or surgical procedure done on the individual

Apart from the above Identification of the victim is another important aspect of the Medical Examiners. They utilize multiple techniques to identify victims' age, race, and sex. Identification of the victim is done by applying various methods like[20]

- DNA Profiling
- Fingerprint Examination
- Examining for tattoos or any body piercing
- Identifying the anatomy of skeletal remains
- Skull and Pelvic remains are used to identify the gender of the individual
- Heel measurement is done to approximately determine the height of the individual
- Skin complexion identification, Eye Color, and Hair Color are analyzed to determine the race
- The age of the victim can be determined by examining tooth development, ossification of bones, etc.

Forensic Odontology or Forensic Dentistry is also highly utilized by the crime department to identify victims. Radiographic examination of dental findings can help to determine the identity of a person. The finds by the odontologists are based upon the degree of formation of root and crown, stage of the eruption of the teeth, and intermixture of primary & adult teeth. These findings are analyzed and small variations in tooth formations help in the identification of the individual at a crime scene.

FORENSIC CHEMISTS

Forensic Chemistry is another stream of Forensic science where the expertise analyzes non-biological compounds found at the scene of the crime. Forensic Chemists cover a wide range of experts who perform arson investigation, drug analysis, DNA analysis, etc. Forensic Chemists link the organic and inorganic substances found at the crime scene to the individual who may have committed the crime.

Forensic chemists utilize various qualitative and quantitive techniques to identify the presence of chemical substances at a crime scene. They use techniques like mass spectroscopy, gas chromatography, High-Performance Liquid Chromatography,

Neutron Activation Analysis, Atomic Absorption Spectroscopy, etc. to determine food adulteration, arson accelerants, toxins, etc[22]

CONCLUSION:

Crime Scene Investigation is highly in need of experts to evaluate, assess, and hasten the process of finding the culprit. Crime Scenes can be anything from physical crime scenes to digital space where cyber forensics experts come into play to identify digital crimes. Apart from the major technicians explained in the context there exists various other dimensions in forensic science like forensic psychology, forensic anthropology, environmental and soil forensic experts, and more. These experts are not availed frequently but are also important in deducing a crime scene. The major technicians performing the task of recreating the crime scene and helping the investigators to identify the perpetrators are thoroughly explained. Expert analysis and evidence are currently been highly admitted in the court of law to identify the suspect and to interpret the crime. Forensic Science is dynamic and is ever evolving. Investigators should utilize the cornucopia of technicians present in the field to hastily solve a crime and to rightly identify the perpetrator.

REFERENCE

1. RICHARD SAFERSTEIN, FORENSIC SCIENCE from the crime scene to the crime lab 4,5 & 8 (2nd Ed, 2018)
2. RICHARD SAFERSTEIN & TIFFANY ROY, AN INTRODUCTION TO FORENSIC SCIENCE, 31-38(13th Ed 2021)
3. *Ibid 2*
4. HOWARD A HARRIS & HENRY C LEE, INTRODUCTION TO FORENSIC SCIENCE & CRIMINALISTICS, 73-74,76 (2nd Ed 2019)
5. ROBERT R OGLE & SHARON PLOTKIN, CRIME SCENE INVESTIGATION & RECONSTRUCTION, 4-5,7 (4th Ed 2018)
6. RICHARD SAFERSTEIN & TIFFANY ROY, AN INTRODUCTION TO FORENSIC SCIENCE, 129 (13th Ed 2021)
7. RICHARD SAFERSTEIN & TIFFANY ROY, AN INTRODUCTION TO FORENSIC SCIENCE, 129 (13th Ed 2021)

8. RICHARD SAFERSTEIN & TIFFANY ROY, AN INTRODUCTION TO FORENSIC SCIENCE, 130 (13th Ed 2021)

9. DR.SURAT P, *FINGERPRINT ANALYSIS IN FORENSIC SCIENCE*, (OCT 28, 2020), Fingerprint Analysis in Forensic Science (azolifesciences.com)

10. A SIMPLIFIED GUIDE TO FINGERPRINT ANALYSIS, Fingerprint Analysis: How It's Done (forensicsciencesimplified.org)

11. A SIMPLIFIED GUIDE TO FINGERPRINT ANALYSIS, Fingerprint Analysis: How It's Done (forensicsciencesimplified.org)

12. BALLISTICS, Ballistics - Crime Museum

13. BALLISTICS, Ballistics - Crime Museum

14. FORENSIC BALLISTICS: A COMPLETE OVERVIEW, Forensic Ballistics : A Complete Overview - Forensic's blog (forensicfield.blog)

15. FORENSIC BALLISTICS: A COMPLETE OVERVIEW, Forensic Ballistics : A Complete Overview - Forensic's blog (forensicfield.blog)

16. ANDREW R.W JACKSON & JULIE M JACKSON, FORENSIC SCIENCE 216-221,(3rd ED 2011)

17. ANDREW R.W JACKSON & JULIE M JACKSON, FORENSIC SCIENCE 239-246,(3rd ED 2011)

18. DR.K.S.NARAYAN REDDY & DR.O.P.MURTY, THE ESSENTIALS OF FORENSIC MEDICINE AND TOXICOLOGY, (33rd ED, 2014)

19. JASON PAYNE JAMES, RICHARD JONES, STEVEN B KARCH & JHON MANLOVE, SIMPSON'S FORESNIC MEDICINE 32, (13th ED, 2011)

20. DR.K.S.NARAYAN REDDY & DR.O.P.MURTY, THE ESSENTIALS OF FORENSIC MEDICINE AND TOXICOLOGY, (33rd ED, 2014)

21. INTRODUCTION TO FORENSIC CHEMISTRY, Introduction to Forensic Chemistry - Forensics Digest

References

overall references in the book reflect here to whom no specific reference made in the same chapher of the book

1 Docket No. 22607-0-1 *State v. Ryan* [1995] 899 P.2d 825 Wn.App.758

2 Swartz Nico, 'The Judicial Implications of Necrophilia' (2015) ISSN: 2348-0394

<https://www.journalair.com/index.php/AIR/article/ download/18078/33492> accessed 27th September 2022

3 Gajbhiye Jay and Saxena Saransh, 'Questioning the Unpredictibility: A Legal Insight into Necrophilia' (2021) National Social and Legal Research Journal <http://www.nslrj.in/> accessed 26th September 2022

4 Case 501/73 *Locke v. State* [1973] Tenn.Cri. App. 826

5 Supra Note 2.

6 Ms. Vidya Dhere and Others, 'Love of Dead: Conceptual Study of Necrophilia' (2019) 4(1)

IJSSER <http://ijsser.org/more2019.php?id=35> accessed 25th September 2022

7 Neelakshi Bhaskar, 'Necrophilia: Legal Perspective' (2020) 2(2) IJLSI

<https://www.ijlsi.com/volume-ii-issue-ii/> accessed 26th September 2022

8 Rosman Jonathan & Philip Resnick, 'Sexual Attraction to Corpses: A Psychiatric Review of Necrophilia' (1989) 17(2) BAAPL

<https://pubmed.ncbi.nlm.nih.gov/ 2667656/#:~:text=Bull%20AM%20Acad,2)%3A153%2D63

> accessed 26th September 2022

9Anand Kumar Vasudevan & Others, 'Necrophilia: A Study of the Psychoanalysis in the Characteristics of the Offenders who sexually molest the dead' 2019 IJOP

<https://ijop.net/index.php/mlu/article/download/734/688/ 1339> accessed on 26th September 2022

10*Ibid*

11 Supra note 2

12 *Ibid*

13 *Ibid*

14 Supra note 2

15 Docket No. 22607-0-1 *State v. Ryan* [1995] 899 P.2d 825 Wn.App.758

16Tyler Trent Ochoa & Christine Jones, 'Defiling the Dead: Necrophilia and the Law', (1997) SCLDC

<https://digitalcommons.law.scu.edu/cgi/viewcontent.cgi?article=1099&context=facpubs> accessed 27TH September 2022

17 Supra Note 9

18 Paramananda Katara v. Union of India, (1995) 3 SCC 248

19 Ramji Singh Mujeeb v. State of U.P., (2009) 5 ALJ 376

20Amrutha v. State of Kerala, WP(C).No. 16175 of 2012 (V)

21 Navtej Singh Johar v. Union of India, AIR 2018 SC 4321

22 Surendra Koli v. State of U.P., Criminal Appeal No. 2227 OF 2010

23 Akan Saikia akaJaygeswar Saikia v. State of Assam, Criminal Revision 293/2006

24 Mohd. Kamruzzaman v. State of West Bengal, W.P. No.23866(W) of 2013

25 Sunil Kumar v. State of Haryana, CRM-M-11274-2021

About The Authors

- Chitrarekha Bharadwaj:

  Author is LL.M. student at Rajiv Gandhi National University of Law, Patiala, Punjab

- Ravneet Kaur

  Author is working as Assistant at Jeevan Institute, Patiala.

- Prachi Gupta

  Author is LL.M. student at Kurukshetra University.

- Manju Kumari

  Author is a practising Advocate at Punjab and Haryana High Court, Chandigarh

- Muskan Mittal

  Author is BBA- LL.B. (Hons.) Student at The ICFAI University, Jaipur

- Vaishali Yadav

  Author is B.A. LL. B. (Hons.) student at Shambhunath institute of Law, Jhalwa Pryagraj

- Dr. Anju Choudhary

  Author is Assistant Professor (Law) UILS, PU, Chandigarh

- Co-Author- Ms. Mehak

  Author is Research Scholar, PU, Chandigarh.

- Garima Oberoi

  Author is LL.M. Constitutional Law at Amity University, Noida.

- Co-Author: Ankush Garg

  Author is LL.M. Constitutional Law at Amity University, Noida.

www.ingramcontent.com/pod-product-compliance
Lightning Source LLC
Chambersburg PA
CBHW021234130726
47988CB00002B/964